DO YOU DARE BELIEVE
THAT JESUS DID NOT DIE
*ON T*_____

that H_____e son
and th_____. . .
that _____alene,
and Bara_____. . that
He wrote His own autobiography . . .
that He lived to be 80 years old and
died fighting the Romans at Masada
. . . that His remains were finally
buried in 1969 . . . and that the
Russians now have the scroll which
proves these disclosures and have so
informed the Vatican?

These disquieting revelations are not
meant to be accepted on faith. *They
are backed by documentary evidence!*

THE JESUS SCROLL

THE MOST DISTURBING BOOK
ABOUT CHRIST AND
CHRISTIANITY EVER PUBLISHED!

SIGNET and MENTOR Books
of Related Interest

THE
JESUS
SCROLL

Donovan Joyce

①
A SIGNET BOOK
NEW AMERICAN LIBRARY
TIMES MIRROR

Library of Congress Catalog Card Number: 73-10454

SIGNET TRADEMARK REG. U.S. PAT. OFF. AND FOREIGN COUNTRIES
REGISTERED TRADEMARK—MARCA REGISTRADA
HECHO EN CHICAGO, U.S.A.

SIGNET, SIGNET CLASSICS, MENTOR, PLUME AND
MERIDIAN BOOKS
are published by The New American Library, Inc.,
1301 Avenue of the Americas, New York, New York 10019

First Printing, October, 1974

1 2 3 4 5 6 7 8 9

PRINTED IN THE UNITED STATES OF AMERICA

To the memory of the deathless 'thousand' Jewish zealots—men, women and children—who so gloriously and so faultlessly elected to die on their own swords at Masada in Israel on 15 April in the year 73 A.D.

Preface

This is not a book of theology written to be understood only by members of the arcane brotherhood, nor is it an academic's forced publication in order to hold his job; it is a plain man's effort to present facts and opinions in plain language and try to unravel the implications arising from a strange experience in Israel during 1964.

Also it is not a book for the bigoted or the ignorant; most of all, I think, it is intended for and will be most valuable to those who are willing to winnow all 'truths' in order to discover the one grain of the real truth which must exist, even though it be rarer than a navel on Adam.

It has required almost eight years of research, consideration and evaluation, and conscience-weighing, guilt inherited from my forebears, writing and rewriting and considerable sacrifice by all in my family to bring to publication. The facts, such as they are, are true; the conclusions drawn might well be wrong or unjustified but, after all, they are only one man's—as were St. Paul's—and have been honestly arrived at from the available evidence.

One's book is an intensely personal thing, even though hawked in the marketplace. Thank you for wanting to read it; in return, though I might earn either your fury or your contempt, all that I really offer you is a lighted match to the dry tinder of your mind.

Contents

THE
JESUS
SCROLL

Introduction

This is a detective story!

By critically examining the old evidence in the light of new testimony which recently emerged from the Wilderness of Judea, it re-opens a celebrated mystery considered closed for all time some two thousand years ago ... and about which men have argued, fought and bled ever since: Did God raise Jesus of Nazareth from the dead?

It is the opinion of many that the existence of God—no matter how certain that might be—is no more than a theophilosophical speculative opinion that is unsupported by real experience, and that there is therefore valid reason for doubting what His Holiness Pope Leo X is reputed to have called 'that fable of Christ'.

Belief in the Resurrection constitutes the central heart-core of the Christian Faith, which insists that it was an actual historical event, fixed in time and the chimera of no man's imagining.

Almost eighty generations of believers in 'the one true faith' have gone to the grave reasonably confident that there was no possible doubt about the matter; twenty-five per cent of the present world-population eventually will do the same ... and the grave danger now exists that not only will they have been wrong, but that this can be proved!

Strangely enough, most of the probable proof lies more in the old evidence of the gospels than in the new testimony, which merely provided the key clue. Despite the importance of the new archaeological find and the breath-taking implications of its alleged authorship, its contents—so far as they are known—are more confirmatory than revelatory.

It has long been recognised by many independent scholars that the gospels tell two distinct stories concurrently, which are mutually irreconcilable and antagonistic. In one,

1

we have a wraith-like Jesus—the beloved teacher, meek and mild—mouthing utterances claimed to be his actual words, but which turn out to be little more than paraphrases of the words of predecessors. In the other, we have the tough Jesus—devious and wily—scheming away at his clandestine plot to overthrow the rule of Rome to establish the Kindom of God on Earth. It is startling to learn—as we shall—precisely what this obliged Jesus to do, and what it actually meant in the context of 1st century Judean religio-politics, which were inseparable.

The sheer incompatibility of the two 'portraits' makes it unlikely that both are correct, yet there they are and Christianity is stuck with them. How both got into the gospels can best be answered, perhaps, by the suggestion that it was the 'tough' Jesus who was the man of history over whose dramatic story—which included his crucifixion—was superimposed the spiritual Jesus envisioned by the theology that arose after the two collided at the Cross.

The story of what really happened on that long-ago week in Jerusalem—as distinct from what was sincerely believed to have happened—has been staring in the face anyone with enough objectivity to read the gospels with eyes unobscured by what someone has called 'the rose-coloured spectacles of piety'.

Unfortunately, the abandonment of these calls for courage of a special sort which many feel is akin to that required for disrobing in public which, perhaps rightly, is regarded as being 'not quite nice'. There is also supernatural dread, the fear of going to Hell and residual terrors of being seized by the black-hooded familiars of the Inquisition for heresy and blasphemy. Happily, those monstrous men of God are gone—one hopes, for ever—even though they vanished less than one hundred and fifty years ago.

Once the gospels are shorn of all the supernatural nonsense, theological posturings and vanities, philosophical speculations and historical and procedural errors which obscure them—thereby greatly impressing the ignorant and keeping the superstitious cowering in fear—the true facts of the tragic drama emerge with crystal clarity.

The three most important reveal that: 1) the historical Jesus was engaged upon an enterprise—the penalty for which was death—far different from his never defined 'mission', which apparently consisted of nothing more than a dash to the Cross: 2) Jesus was not betrayed but surrendered himself to the Roman authorities in a deal—made through an intermediary—in which Pilate released the 'notable prisoner', Barabbas, in exchange for him: 3) the extremely suspicious circumstances surrounding the entire 'execution' proceedings not only ensured that a living Jesus would emerge from the tomb, but demanded it! In fact, in the circumstances—heavy with the scent of conspiracy—it would have been even more astonishing had he not emerged, than that he had!

It never seems to have occurred to anyone at the time that the most likely explanation of a living man leaving a tomb was that a living man had entered it. Not even Pilate had taken the trouble to more than casually check with a soldier that Jesus was dead and, in view of his likely part in the plot, it can be taken as certain that his enquiry was merely to establish the fact that he had checked. Tiberius Caesar had a long arm!

And so Christianity had its nucleus.

It is not generally understood by Christians that the gospels had nothing at all to do with the actual birth of their religion; their role came much later. In fact, the faith was flourishing in at least a dozen centres in the pagan world outside Judea many years before the very first gospel was written and Paul—the former Saul—was in his grave.

Nor was it even the simple fact that Jesus had emerged from the tomb that had generated the faith. Rather was it the interpretation that was placed on this event several years later by Saul (Paul), the ferocious persecutor of the secondary group of Jesus' 'followers' though, oddly enough, not of his former immediate disciples. This has yet to be satisfactorily explained.

It was impossible for Saul not to have heard rumours about the strange event at the tomb yet it was obvious from his persecutions that he hadn't believed a word of it. Nor, apparently, had the disciples, as their immunity from persecution testifies. However, being an intellectual with the doctrine of a dozen pagan cults at his fingertips, the enigma posed by the tomb gnawed away at his mind on his long journeys to and fro in his sickening trade of Temple bounty-hunter for which he had forsaken tent making. On the road one day, en route to Damascus in search of more victims—ill, no doubt, from his mysterious malady—he suddenly solved the mystery of how a dead man could enter a tomb and a living man leave it. For

Saul, there was only one irrational answer, the Hand of God! Jesus had been the subject of Divine Resurrection! Immediately he had a vision of Jesus . . . and even dialogue with him . . . and fell down blinded by the dazzling light from Heaven. Four days later, as he relates, he was baptized!

From that point, Saul became Paul and Christianity was on its way, hammered out of a synthesis of pagan doctrines well known in the Mediterranean basin and beyond. The area had long been familiar with Suffering Saviours and Redeemers and Paul's casting of Jesus in this role broke so little new ground, in fact, that when he joined the Pantheon Club in Heaven all that old Mithras and Soter and one or two other gods—who died and were resurrected every year—had to do was say 'Hi!' and make room on the bench.

As the gospels came along during the half-century following Paul's death, they naturally reflected not only what was still remembered about the historical Jesus, but what was believed about him by the church to that date. As, by then, Jesus had become the Christ, the Suffering Saviour and Redeemer of Mankind and the Son of God, it is quite certain that anything in the historical Jesus story that conflicted in any doctrinal way with the then-image of Him was discarded. As we shall soon discover, the ability to mangle and distort the truth—even to eliminate or create it—in the cause of theological expediency was not a skill enjoyed exclusively by the gospel authors; their subsequent 'editors' wielded not only deftly censorious pencils but mightily creative and imaginative pens. But, remember, not a jot of it all was intended to deceive, but merely to glorify!

It is this early tendency of the early Church in the first three centuries of its life to trifle with the truth—in short, with history—in the good cause of glorification that has proved an acute embarrassment to its inheritors ever since. It is the knowledge of just how historically insecure the whole edifice of Christian doctrine really is and the extent to which it is vulnerable to the evidence from the past that has made the whole Ecclesiastical Establishment eye the busy spades of history's hand-maidens—the archaeologists—somewhat bleakly and with many a nervous twitch.

The discovery of the astonishing Dead Sea Scrolls a generation ago sent a shudder of apprehension throughout

Christendom. These, if they proved nothing else—which is debatable—at least demonstrated that it was possible for documents written a century before Christ to make an incredible journey through time. Skilful denigratory footwork by influential Christian scholars—whom only the most naive would have expected to have worshipped truth more than doctrine—swiftly bled away the importance of their implications vis-a-vis the faith. Today they amount to little more than ancient literary curiosities. However, they still exist and in their potential to key-in with some future discovery pose a constant threat to Christianity's claim to both originality and full historicity.

Nor is the threat as insignificant or innocuous as it might seem. There are more than one thousand two hundred ruined cities, towns and villages in Israel and Jordan—formerly part of Judea—and more than half of these are dotted like a rash along the banks of the river Jordan, where both Jesus and his cousin, John the Baptiser, were active. It was in this area, in fact, where they had a bitter quarrel—played down in the gospels—which led to John's death and Jesus' triumph and glorification. Only about ten per cent of these ruins have been explored by the spade so who can say what evidence embarrassing to Christianity and annihilating of some important doctrinal 'truth' might not yet be turned up? Imagine the havoc that would be caused should it ever be proved that the quarrel between the cousins was really a sordid battle for power, riches . . . and the Throne of Israel.

Or, something more likely, proof of the assertion of a solid body of scholarship that 'Jesus of Nazareth' could never have been known by his name, for the excellent reason, one would think, that Nazareth did not then exist.

Aware of the potential danger of the spade, the Ecclesiastical Establishment might already have started preparing the faithful for the day when the rock of historicity might have to be exchanged for the quicksands of pure theology. In the early sixties the then Dean of St. Paul's in London made an astonishing statement: 'I see no reason to suppose that a complete abandonment of the historical basis for Christianity would necessarily involve the end of the religion.' Not all Christians would go along with that . . . unless there was no choice. Even while the optimistic Dean was uttering those shattering words history was getting ready, perhaps to put them to the test.

A document which makes absurd all claims to the historicity of the Ascension—which the Church still claims to have been physical, Newton not withstanding—was nestling beneath a pile of ancient rubble in a ruin in the Wilderness of Judea, where it had lain since 15 April in the year 73 A.D.

The nonsense it makes of the Ascension myth can, possibly, also be extended to that keystone in the arch of Christian faith, the Resurrection. If so, it is a veritable 'time-bomb' for Christianity and, in 1961, it was on its final countdown of almost nineteen centuries.

On a day in November, three years later, it 'exploded' . . . and this book is the 'fall-out'.

Melbourne 1972

D. M. J.

1 / The Fifteenth Scroll

On the night of Monday 14 December 1964, an archaeologist whom I had known for the past ten days as Professor Max Grosset—a name which he cheerfully admitted was false—accosted me at Tel-Aviv's Lod Airport with the offer of $5000 if I would perform a 'small service'.

All that I had to do was smuggle out of Israel that very night—aboard BOAC's Flight 710 to Australia—an ancient parchment scroll which he claimed to have stolen, several weeks earlier, from the excavations of biblical King Herod the Great's ruined fortress of Masada, on the western shore of the Dead Sea.

What robbed the clearly illegal caper of most of its simple charm was that the bag containing the precious document had to be brazenly smuggled past two gimlet-eyed security men—thought to have been from the Israeli Department of Antiquities—posted at the door to the tarmac, specifically to intercept both this scroll and its carrier.

It was at Masada that the Jewish Rebellion against Roman rule and occupancy exploded in 66 A.D. when several thousand tough Galilean Zealots massacred the garrison and seized the fortress. From here, it had fanned out east and north and the embers of rebellion burst into the flames of war. The Zealots were fanatical Loyalists and Messianists and were determined on one of their periodic bids to restore the throne of the Maccabean kings usurped by Herod the Great a century before and which, on his death, vanished down the maw of Roman greed.

Splitting their forces in two, one group stayed at Masada while the other—with the pretender, Mennahem, at its head—marched on Jerusalem in the hope of capturing the Holy City and its Temple for God. The attempt failed; many were killed—including Mennahem—and the survivors fled back to Masada.

7

Pouring in the Legions, Rome savagely struck back, devastating the land of milk and honey from 'Dan to Beersheba'. Four years later—with at least a million dead and as many more enslaved; with Jerusalem and the Temple destroyed and the country a bloody, smoking ruin—the war was over.

Except at Masada.

Despite the obvious collapse of their plans, the Zealots spurned Rome's offer to spare their lives and stubbornly refused to lay down their arms and quit. It took a further three years, a vast amount of money, a whole Legion of 6000 troops and the prodigious labour of 15,000 Jewish slaves to overwhelm them—a mere 1,000 men, women and children.

It proved, in the event, to have been the definitive pyrrhic victory. When the exultant Romans burst into the fortress, they found only corpses and sullenly drifting smoke. Preferring death to enslavement, the Zealots had first set Masada ablaze, then killed each other.

Such, in bare outline, is the account left to posterity by the Jewish historian—and Roman apologist—Josephus, who was both a Jewish General and a Roman sycophant, if nothing worse. There is now very good reason to suspect that Josephus might have misrepresented the Zealots' motive for their sublime sacrifice.

In 1964 Masada was being 'dug' by a massive archaeological expedition led by the distinguished Israeli scholar and soldier, General Yigael Yadin, under the auspices of the Israeli Department of Antiquities and, apparently, also under an extremely tight security screen. Financed by wealthy overseas patrons, the expedition was staffed by a group of brilliant experts in various fields and was 'muscled' by thousands of volunteers who, at their own expense, had made their way to Herod's ancient lair from all over the world.

And the author? The prospect of securing a mass of authentic background material for an historical novel already on the stocks—and promised for early delivery to a New York publisher—tempted me into mortgaging my house in order to make my pilgrimage. It was a disastrous decision which, almost eight years later, is still bitterly regretted.

On arrival, General Yadin refused me a permit to visit the site, which was swarming with some six hundred people of all kinds, backgrounds, professions and nationalities. Despite the intervention of Mr Menachem Begin, present leader of the Gahal Party in the Israeli Knesset (parliament), and of the then Prime Minister—the late Mr Levi Eshkol—the General remained mysteriously obdurate and refused to reverse his decision. I was not to learn until later that, from the night of my arrival in the country, I had been under some suspicion of being involved in the theft of an object of antiquity from Masada, and was under surveillance. It is, one hopes, unnecessary to say that I was entirely innocent of any wrongdoing.

The Yadin Expedition's discoveries were of sensational importance and included no fewer than *fourteen* parchment scrolls—or considerable portions of them—which had lain in the dry soil of Masada for almost two thousand years. One of these provided a definite link between the Zealots and the Essene seminarians of Qumran—thirty miles to the north of Masada—where the famous Dead Sea Scrolls had been found in the late forties.

It might be recalled that these contained so many startling parallels and inexplicable similarities between the Essenes and the early Christians—whom the former predated by at least a full century—that many New Testament scholars, becoming alarmed at the implications, denounced the scrolls as fakes and refused to examine them or even to acknowledge their existence.

When informed by me—by letter from Australia—of Grosset and his claim to have discovered and stolen a 'fifteenth scroll' at Masada, General Yadin swiftly dismissed the story as 'fantastic nonsense' and gratuitously undertook to 'prove' it should he ever be asked to comment on this book. Not only would I not avoid his challenge but I should welcome it; in fact, the very first witness I should call to support my case would be General Yadin, himself.

Not only is he an expert on scrolls and the conditions under which—and in which—they have so far been found, but he has had some experience of the 'stolen' variety. He it was who, when four of the most valuable of the Dead Sea Scrolls had been 'liberated' to the U.S.A. by a larcenous Christian Archbishop, acquired them for the nation of Israel for a reputed $250,000. That, legally, they were the property of the Kingdom of Jordan doesn't seem to have occurred to anyone, or if it did, to have worried them unduly.

Taking this as a guide and knowing that, additionally, any sort of scroll in 1950 was worth somewhere about $15.00 per square inch, sight unseen—and you had to be quick, otherwise it smartly went to the next museum or scholar in the queue—the scroll which I was asked to smuggle out of Israel on that December night might have been worth a great deal of money. The bribe money offered would seem to suggest that this was realised by the thief who found it. In view of his identification of the scroll's author, the document might well be priceless. This apart, there can be no other ancient document in the world which can be more precisely dated.

According to Professor Grosset—and I have only his word for my meagre knowledge of the scroll's alleged contents—it had been written on the night of 15 April 73 A.D. However, as the orthodox Jewish 'day' begins at sunset and ends at the same time twenty-four hours later, the night of 15 April would correspond with 14 April, according to the way non Jews count the hours and measure the days.

The Roman battering ram had breached the fortress gate just as the sun had set and, because they never fought at night—when hand-to-hand combat was impossible—the X Legion ceased operations until dawn. So, as the scroll author reports both the battering-down of the gate and the Roman withdrawal, it must have been during the ensuing thirteen hours of darkness that—as the Romans sharpened their swords for the work of the morrow—the author had penned his scroll. By dawn, he was dead!

And his name?

Again according to Professor Grosset, the man had written his name: *'Yeshua ben Ya'akob ben Gennesareth'* and described himself as 'son of eighty years'. But he had added the astonishing information that he was the last rightful inheritor of the Hasmonean (Maccabean) Kings of Israel.

Equally astonishing—at least to me—was the news that his name, when translated into English, was: 'Jesus of Gennesareth, son of Jacob'.

Because of its familiar ring, no doubt, it came as no great surprise when Grosset claimed that this man was identical with 'Jesus of Nazareth' whose name would appear to lack only the Hebrew prefix *'Gen'* (garden) to become identical to that of the scroll author. This would hardly seem to be enough on which to base any firm identification so that, apparently, the document would seem to have contained further information sufficient to justify Grosset's finding.

It will be recalled that Jesus of Nazareth allowed himself to be addressed as King of Israel and that whether or not he was had been discussed by him and Pilate at his trial. In fact, it was for this crime—heinous to the Romans because it challenged the supremacy of the Emperor Tiberius—that Jesus was arrested, tried, convicted and sentenced to death by crucifixion.

Gennesareth was one of history's several names for the Sea of Galilee but, specifically, it was applied to the small but exquisite and fertile plain—described as a veritable 'garden of princes', which the name might mean—which sparkled like a jewel of abundance on the lake's western shore just south of Capernaum. The gospels rather curiously describe this as Jesus' 'own city', which carries the strong connotation of ownership by inheritance—much as some of Britain's aristocracy own villages and small towns today—rather than that Jesus had merely lived there. The Plain of Gennesareth bore many towns and one of these, Magdala, is thought to have been the home of Mary Magdalene—which might or might not have been significant. Another was 'Arimeh'—since vanished with all traces—and the possibility that this was home to a very prominent gospel character will be discussed later.

To have been about 80 in 73 A.D. would have required that the scroll—Jesus' year of birth was 7 B.C., which, according to one reckoning, and if the story of Herod's slaughter of the innocents is to be believed, must have been also the year of the gospel-Jesus' birth. It certainly seems remarkable that there should have been two men named Jesus, living at the same time, who both claimed to King of Israel and to have had some connection with Gennesareth sufficient to justify their names incorporating an allusion to it. The suggestion that, originally, Jesus might have been 'of Gennesareth' instead of merely 'of Nazareth' is given added weight by the insistence of some scholars that, in those days, the town of Nazareth simply did not exist. The fact of Nazareth and 'Nesareth—we omit the prefix—being spelled differently need worry nobody.

The only other piece of information given me about the

scroll author that might seem to conflict with the known Jesus is the claim that he was the son of *Ya'kob* or Jacob. As will be shown, this provides no difficulty, for a child of no known human parentage might have owned to a paternal Jacob as easily as to God. In the event, however, we can even point to Jesus' actual father, for the gospels identify him.

As to the rest of the information supplied by Professor Grosset—and it was a necessarily hurried discussion held, actually, in the men's lavatory at the airport—it consists of one meagre fact; that the scroll author had a son and, therefore, had been married. This son, whose name was not given me, had actually been crucified before his father's eyes. Lacking the details doesn't prevent us from guessing that this had occurred at Masada. It was, in fact, an often used device by the Romans to force a city's surrender. Capturing some notable from the city they would pretend to crucify him so that, touched by horror—a crucified man was thought to be cursed by God—and pity, the citizens would throw open the gates. If they did not, the execution would proceed in earnest. It is impossible not to think that this might have happened at Masada just below the gate through which the Romans eventually poured.

Because a son requires a mother, if the theory of the congruity of the two Jesuses is to be consolidated, reasonable evidence that the gospel-Jesus was married will have to be produced. It is believed that this can be done, not only by the argument that Jesus—whatever it was that theology later envisioned him to have been—was fully human and, as such, was subject to exactly the same laws and social customs as other Jews of his time, but also by direct evidence in the gospels. That her name was Mary is certain, and that she was the same Mary called Magdalene, is almost so.

As was said earlier, the 'fifteenth scroll' confirms more than it reveals and, essentially, its role would appear to be that of a key in a lock, whose turning enables us to open the door leading to the historical Jesus and, at last, to discover with reasonable certainty exactly what his real mission might have been. It was this which led to the Cross—not his inferred mission which the gospels fiddle around with but never actually describe. It must never be forgotten that the historical Jesus was sent to the Cross for breaking a Roman law—claiming to be King of Israel—or that the crime upon which he is alleged to have been arrested (blasphemy) was not an offence in Roman eyes, however seriously it was regarded by the Sanhedrin, which was the supreme court of Judea. To paraphrase the aphorism concerning equality, in Judea some were more supreme than others and the Sanhedrin had to bend the knee to Rome, through the person of the Governor, Pontius Pilate.

Although the scroll was sighted only briefly and its alleged contents—as passed on here—are no more than hearsay, not even its existence is essential to the drawing of a much more likely portrait of the historical Jesus than is given by the gospels. Though all the necessary elements and details are there, they have to be unscrambled and wiped clean of the thick, diffusing layer of stardust that's been sprinkled over them as theology's interest waned in the man who had lived, in inverse proportion to its need of a God who had died ... in order to live.

Having made its brief appearance the scroll, apparently, has since vanished. Not only has no word of it appeared in any medium, but alarming threats have been made in an endeavour to ensure that none would appear in book form.

The most overt of these followed within four hours of my seeking the aid of the Honorable Walter Jonas, member of the Legislative Council of Victoria, to solve the Masada ban mystery. After a long discussion with him at State Parliament House, at which he offered to make enquiries on my behalf in Israel, I returned home just in time to take an anonymous phone call. The guttural voice told me that my contact with Jonas had been noted, and that I'd be stupid to pursue the matter. 'Knock it off!' warned the caller, 'You've got a family, remember!' He hung up ... and I 'knocked it off'. Since then, I've had no contact with Walter Jonas nor—to be Irish—has he had any with me. As I said earlier, there have been other and more frightening threats but, for what one hopes will be obvious reasons, one doesn't wish to go into details.

Though the origin of these is merely suspected, they have been made and must have been issued on behalf of 'someone' having a vested interest in preventing this book's publication. Where is the 'fifteenth scroll' now? While it would be outrageous to say, positively, that it is in the possession of any particular person or government, it is extremely odd that events since the scroll was last seen heading in a particular nation's direction—less than ninety minutes flight from its border—would seem to suggest not only where it now is, but also the use to which it is being put. Should this be so, then it can be taken as certain that expert opinion considers it both authentic and a potentially devastating threat to Christianity.

The uncorroborated testimony of any witness, rightly, is entitled to be regarded with suspicion. This fact of life is accepted without resentment; after all, it's merely par for the course. However, in the circumstances it is unfortunate that one did not have recorders and a camera-crew handy to record the incident. While discussing credibility, it is worth keeping well in mind that there have been at least two celebrated instances of even less credible events being accepted as gospel truth on the word of an uncorroborated witness. One involved a mentally-disturbed reputed ex-harlot called Mary Magdalene, while the other was Saul of Tarsus, whose account of the miraculous incident which inspired him to become the architect of Christianity, clearly indicates that we are dealing with a religious psychotic. Presented here in affidavit style, it is based on the relevant parts of Chapters 8 and 9 of *Acts*. Read and ponder well.

TESTAMENT

I, Saul of Tarsus, formerly an arresting officer of the Heretics, Schismatists & Sectaries Squad attached to the Holy Temple of Jerusalem under the general authority of the Sanhedrin and under the special authority of Gamaliel the Rabban, do testify:

After the death of Stephen to which I was consenting, there arose a great persecution of the Church which was at Jerusalem and they were all scattered abroad throughout the regions of Judea and Samaria, except the Apostles.

As for me, I made havoc of the church, entering into every house and haling men and women, committed them to prison. Therefore they that were scattered abroad went everywhere preaching the word.

And I, yet breathing out threatenings and slaughter against the disciples of the Lord, went unto the High Priest and desired of him letters to Damascus to the synagogues that I found any of this way, whether they were men or women, I might bring them bound, to Jerusalem.

And as I journeyed, I came near to Damascus, and

suddenly there shined around me a great light from Heaven. I fell to earth and heard a voice saying unto me: 'Saul, why persecutest thou me?' And I said: 'Who art thou Lord' And the Lord said: 'I am Jesus, whom thou persecutest; it is hard for you to kick against the pricks' And I, trembling and astonished, said: 'Lord, what wilt thou have me do?' And the Lord said unto me: 'Arise! And go into the city, and it shall be told thee what thou must do!' And the men which journeyed with me stood speechless, hearing a voice, but seeing no man. And I arose from the earth, and when my eyes were opened, I saw no man, but they led me by the hand and brought me to Damascus. And I was there three days without sight, and neither did eat nor drink.

On the fourth day cometh Ananias whom I had seen in a vision, putting his hands on me that I might receive my sight. And Ananias cometh and put his hands on me and immediately there fell from my eyes as it had been scales and I received my sight forthwith, and arose, and was baptised.

(Signed) Saul of Tarsus, now
a believer in the Lord Jesus.

Quite apart from the interesting fact that God's Revelation did not include that of the speaker's identity, so that Saul had to ask, that was the 'evidence' upon which he—at last and after several years of obvious disbelief in the Resurrection—finally came to accept its historicity and, on this in turn, founded the faith which, today, has 800,000,-000 adherents who have accepted Saul's uncorroborated evidence without question.

And so we turn to those 'Divinely Inspired' books of the faith—the gospels—which, whatever they might be, are not the gospel truth and, as they stand today, are in part probably the greatest literary frauds and fakes ever foisted on to the credulous generations of the earth for almost two thousand years.

2 / But Are They the Gospel Truth?

It is a chilling thought that had the author lived in Spain a mere hundred and fifty years ago, this book could not have been written without his life being, quite literally, at stake.

Although scepticism was already stirring in other parts of the 'civilised' world where the fearsome Inquisition had fallen into a decline, those who challenged the accuracy of the gospels still had to walk with care. In Spain those monstrous men of God still ran a pretty tight torture chamber until, in 1816, the use of torture to force heretics to confess was forbidden by the Pope. Eighteen years later—bowing to the inevitable—His Holiness disbanded the Inquisition and, after some six hundred years, Europe could at last breathe clean air, untainted by the stench of burning corpses.

No longer awed by the sinister greasy, black stains in a thousand marketplaces where heretics had writhed at the stake for 'the glory of the Lord Jesus Christ', thinking men all over Europe began to wonder was the Truth expounded by the gospels literally the historical truth.

Did it all really happen?

Or only some of it?

Or any of it?

Sniffing like bloodhounds, at a trail gone cold when the inhabitants of Britain still wore skins and painted their faces with woad, the doubting and the downright sceptical—lacking any real 'bench-mark' from which to measure the historical Jesus—were trying to pinion their man with ropes of sand.

As, one by one, they got their hands on Whiston's English translation of The Jewish War by Flavius Josephus—until then only sparsely available in Greek—they were suddenly transported to ancient Judea and, at last, received their first comprehension of those times and

16

of the great social, political and religious ferments which had turned the country into a frenzied ant heap.

Clearly, it was against this background that the historical Jesus would have to be seen, yet the gospels gave little or no hint of the turmoil of the times and, indeed, seemed to suspend him in the air free of all human events that must have been taking place, under his very nose. However, once the sceptics and the curious had this missing background and could hear the grinding gears of history as it was, their mutterings and whisperings became a great shout of doubt.

Ever since, bitter battles have been fought between the orthodox dogmatist theologians, and the sceptical scholars and historians who have dared challenge the alleged historicity of the gospel events . . . and even the authenticity of those books. The doubt spread from the colleges and universities to people so alarmingly that—as only one example—in 1870 the Christian Evidence Society had to be formed to counteract the current forms of unbelief among the educated classes of England.

Claiming that the gospels—to a great extent—are an unreliable hotchpotch of Messianic hysteria, myth and legend, with a thin smear of historical and biographical recollections on top, the sceptics go so far as to charge that even events which might have been true, have been so distorted to suit changing theological and doctrinal requirements that, as they stand, they are now historical to only a limited extent.

How far are these charges true?

Temporarily putting aside such obvious instances as the two 'true' genealogies of Jesus and the impossibly irreconcilable dates of his birth—and the equally-obvious borrowings from pagan religions, Judaistic sects and Greek mythology and philosophy, the charges must be removed from areas of mere suspicion to those where proof is possible.

It will probably come as a traumatic shock to the devout to learn at last something which the Church has known for centuries, that *the last twelve verses of the final chapter of the gospel of Mark are bogus.*

Almost as shocking to Christians will be the knowledge that both disputing factions of scholarship unanimously agree that these bogus verses were never part of the original *Mark* and can be no more than fraudulent additions—made with whatever motive—by some unknown 'editor' at some equally unknown time.

The seriousness of the revelation lies in the fact that it is these verses which provide the very first gospel report of the Resurrection and of the risen Jesus' supposed appearances.

The alarming consequences, however, cannot be restricted to *Mark,* which is generally thought and accepted to have been the first of the four gospels written. Both *Luke* and *Matthew* plundered the first gospel for much of their own material—the latter stealing whole sections verbatim—so that there exists a strong probability that they might also have stolen the Resurrection story or that, like that of *Mark,* theirs are also editorial insertions.

So, at least to this extent, the sceptic's case would appear to have been proved and, as their opponents agree, we must accept the verdict as final.

In this case then—with the possible exception of Paul's narrative in *Corinthians* (1st) chapter 15—we have no absolutely reliable evidence that, historically, the Resurrection ever occurred so that complete belief in the event must depend on faith alone. While this might be what religion is all about, the fact that the accounts of the event which lie at the heart-core of Christianity are, in fact, bogus, waters the currency of the faith which has resolutely claimed to have been founded on provable historical events. More than this, the failure of the Church to ensure that all adherents fully understood both the position and the implications, seriously damages its credibility and its proclamation of the Truth.

A further example of the same kind in which a known bogus addition to a gospel was given the same 'Quick! Under the rug!' treatment is *John* 8:1-11 which relates the incident of Jesus and the woman taken in adultery.

For at least a century it has been known that these verses, too, were bogus insertions yet the parable is still repeatedly trotted out from ten thousand pulpits as an example of Jesus' wisdom, charity and mercy. The tale is absent from *all* the most ancient manuscripts and also from the Syriac, Coptic and Armenian versions. It was unknown to any Christian writer before—significantly—Ambrose (340-397 A.D.) and, as an added reason for a great Ecclesiastical blush, some codices leave it out of the gospel of *John* . . . only to include it in *Luke!* Perhaps, like the author, you are wondering how that could happen in 'Divinely Inspired' works.

A still further example—which, perhaps, the author is bringing to notice for the first time—is the famous story of the risen Jesus and Doubting Thomas in *John* 20: 19-31.

If this clearly contrived tale of the supernatural is to be accepted as true, then we must reject the same gospel's account of the Crucifixion, to which John claims to have been an eye-witness; certainly his stark reporting of that event inspires more confidence than does his alleged account of Jesus oozing through solid walls. That it was complete nonsense and not in accord with the facts can be shown by a description of crucifixion as it brutally was.

The Romans used two quite different methods which were never combined, and whose employment depended on what, apart from the victim's death, was desired as an additional bonus by the State. They might best be described as 'fast' and 'slow'. Although death was the ultimate objective of both methods, the 'slow' was designed to inflict hideous suffering as well, on any particularly offensive criminal such as anyone guilty of treason. These poor wretches took up to six days to expire. Fitting a horn or saddle to the upright so that it projected between the victim's legs at the crotch and supported his body weight, they then nailed his wrists to the crossbar and left him for shock, pain, humiliating nakedness, starvation, thirst and the mockery of passers-by to finish off.

With the 'fast' method, however, used when it was more a case of speed than the infliction of unbearable pain almost infinitely prolonged, the horn was replaced by a tiny platform on which the doomed man stood, preferably on the balls of his feet. Now, instead of the wrists being nailed they were bound to the crossbar by leather thongs. Except for the strain of standing in that fashion, shame at his nakedness and the knowledge that death was only a couple of hours away, he was in no great distress or pain. When it came time to kill him, the executioner resorted to the *crucifragium,* a club-like horror with which he broke the legs. Deprived of their support, the body sagged and the entire weight was thrown upon the thongs, which promptly proceeded to strangle the circulation. In about an hour, it has been reckoned, paralysis, suffocation and heart-failure brought the execution to a merciful end.

From the description of what happened at Golgotha—
as reported in the gospel of *John*—it is quite evident that
Jesus was crucified by the 'fast' method. The legs of the
two thieves were broken by the executioner who, coming
to do the same to Jesus was astonished to find him already
dead. Additional evidence to make it a certainty that Jesus
was executed in this way lies in the fact that sunset and
so, the Sabbath—this one also being the Passover being
doubly sacred—was a mere three hours away when the
Crucifixion began. Under no circumstances would the Romans—who strictly observed Jewish law in this regard—
permit a crucified man to hang on a cross into a Sabbath.
So, contrary to what has long been believed, Jesus was not
nailed to the Cross, he was bound.

Yet, in the Doubting Thomas fairytale, we are presented with a risen Jesus who not only bears nail-holes in his
'hands', but invites the sceptical disciple to stick his finger
in them . . . which, we are told, he *does!*

In the circumstances we cannot do other than regard
the whole Doubting Thomas episode as a most flagrant example of gospel falsification. Strangely enough, it is entirely to this bogus passage in the gospel of *John* that we
owe the generally held belief that Jesus was nailed to the
Cross when, as has been shown! he was not.

But even worse is to come!

The sad truth is that the four gospels that we have today might not be—probably *are* not—exactly the same
four of the same names that were used throughout the
Church during most of the first three centuries of the
Christian era.

Though diligent search has been made for many years
and hundreds of ancient churches, monasteries and other
likely repositories ransacked, the queer fact is that not one
gospel manuscript any older than some time in the 4th
century has even been found. Not even the Vatican, with
its reported *twenty-five miles of documents*, has ever produced a copy any 'younger', which is not quite the same as
saying that none exists.

We evidently owe this alarming fact to the Emperor
Constantine who, having become a convert to Christianity,
soon made his new faith the official religion of the Roman
Empire, which he ruled from ancient Byzantium, renamed
Constantinople. And so, at about 320 A.D. the Church not
only came to glorious power but was given a clearly God-

sent opportunity to revenge itself on the descendants of those who had persecuted it for almost three hundred years. Unleashing a reign of terror on those pagans who stubbornly refused the new faith, Constantine and the Church waded deep in blood and apparently enjoyed the experience, for the lions enjoyed pagans as much as they had Christians and the crosses now carried different victims.

At that time, the various churches were autonomous under their own Bishops and doctrine—and, perhaps, even dogma—differed from church to church according to the personal theological views of each Bishop. These were evolved from the large variety of gospels then in circulation, of which those of *Matthew, Mark, Luke* and *John* were only an important section. It was this importance, or acceptability, which resulted in them being admitted to the Canon, which meant that they were considered to have been divinely inspired, a somewhat naive concept in view of what was later done to them.

In addition to the four Canonical gospels, there was a larger group, called the Apocrypha—meaning 'hidden'—which the church admitted to its Canon but which the Protestant schismatists would later deny entry to theirs.

A third, and intriguing, group of gospels seems to have had no classification except that they were regarded as being less authentic, authoritative or edifying than the others. In point of fact, some of the despised gospels are no less authentic than the received and, in several cases, might be even more so. Indeed, one of them was long used by the Church before being quietly discarded.

In its early years the Church was a great scavenger of writings suitable for its purpose, irrespective of their origin. However, no writer reached the churchly eminence or distinction of Virgil—who died about fifty years before the rise of Christianity—who was not only regarded as one of the prophets but whose name was actually embodied in the ritual of the early Church. Copies of his 'Aeneid' were used in even the most anti-pagan monasteries as a book of prophecy, or of ecclesiastical fortune-telling. Opening the book at random, the first line to strike the eye was considered as a prediction of the future. So, with this sort of thing going on, it is no wonder that the various Bishops evolved a strange variety of concepts about the 'true' nature of Jesus. Some saw him

as Divine and the Son of God, while others recoiled from
such a pagan and blasphemous view. Still others sat on
the fence of indecision harvesting their splinters.

Alarmed at the schisms that threatened to tear the
Church apart, Constantine convoked the Council of Nicea
in 325 A.D. and demanded that the assembled Bishops
should end their squabbles and decide, once and for all,
who and what Jesus had been, and his true nature.

Incredibly, a ballot was held and in a vote which wasn't
unanimous, be it noted, it was decided that Jesus was truly
Divine and the Son of God. Surely he was the first God
ever elected to the Seat of Heaven by the democratic process!

As 'Son of God' was merely one of the several euphemisms for the Jewish office of Messiah—which, in turn,
was a euphemism for 'King of Israel'—the Christian Bishops thus took a Jewish historical fact and distorted it so
that it produced an implied *physical* relationship with God,
who was then promptly seen by the masses of the faithful
as an old man with a long, grey beard. This wasn't the
Council's intent but that's what got through to 'the man
in the pew' and has remained one of the great Christian
hangups ever since.

It is at this point that a daring, but probable, explanation can be put forward to explain why it is that no gospel
manuscript any earlier than the 4th century exists, although we have a few inconsequential fragments.

In 331 A.D.—six years after the Council of Nicea's incredible ballot—Constantine 'caused to be prepared under
the direction of the noted Church historian, Eusebius, *fifty*
copies of the gospels for use in the churches of Byzantium'. That there was a great deal more involved than
seems inplicit in that laconic footnote to history becomes
apparent after a little probing.

Firstly, why were fifty copies necessary? Were there so
many churches in the city of Byzantium? One is inclined
to doubt it. For that matter, why were any copies necessary? Had all the gospel books or manuscripts in use until
then, suddenly—and simultaneously—worn out? It is, of
course, possible though highly unlikely. Moreover, if fresh
copies were required, why should the Emperor of the Roman Empire have personally concerned himself with what,
after all and on the face of it, was merely a simple book
order? And if only facsimiles were involved, why was this

task of merely copying—usually performed by scribes employed for this particular purpose—so important that the great historian and scholar, Eusebius, had to supervise the project? And how are we to define 'prepared'?

We look at our gospels as they now stand and remember that, even though the last of them, *John*, was written more than two hundred years before the Council of Nicea had decided by a show of hands that Jesus was the Son of God and Divine, somehow or other these sacred books just happen to contain the new theological concepts evolved two centuries later.

Is the vanishing gospels mystery to be solved by the implications of Constantine's directive to Eusebius? It is certainly curious that we should have lost *every one* of the many copies of the gospels—possibly hundreds—in the use in the churches right up until the very time that Eusebius produced his new edition.

Is it reasonable to suggest that, as this occurred within six years of the Council of Nicea, the *old* gospels might have been recalled . . . and destroyed, to be replaced by the new which, naturally enough, presented Jesus in a totally new light? With him now the Son of God and Divine, Christianity clearly had little further use for the historical man, who now was draped in the glorious vestments of celestial theology. And so it might have been that superfluous or clashing biographical details were eliminated, to be replaced by 'events' designed to support the very doctrine that had actually evolved them. Clearly, it was the cart that pulled the horse!

Equally clearly, the religion's rationale had shifted from the man to the God. The locus of interest was no longer the Earth, but Heaven . . . and the Holy City, Golgotha, and the Empty Tomb were but steps in the glorious stairway built, not by a humble carpenter but by a tent-maker, reaching all the way up to the stars!

3 / Nazareth—the Phantom City

Contrary to what might be expected, there is no intention of claiming that the 'fifteenth scroll', allegedly written by Jesus of Gennesareth, is an authentic relic of the 1st century A.D., only that it might be. It might, in fact, be just as bogus as parts of the gospels have been shown to be. In any case, it is a matter for the scholars, archaeologists and others to argue over when, as it must eventually, it finally emerges into the light of day. When that day will be is anybody's guess.

However, that does not prevent pursuit of the possibility that, historically, Jesus of Gennesareth and his story might have provided the basic character and events for the original gospel story; in short, that he might have been the man known to the world as Jesus of Nazareth.

As has been stated earlier, the likelihood that there never was a 'Jesus of Nazareth' is based on the extremely strong suspicion that no such town as Nazareth existed in those times. Just how good is the evidence to support this opinion?

Although it is always dangerous to accept what is known as 'evidence from silence', it must be granted that in the case against Nazareth's existence in the 1st century A.D., the silence is eloquent.

Consulted about the existence of any kind of Judean settlement called Nazareth, history coldly turns her back and remains silent for several hundred years until, in the first written record so far discovered—a 5th century Jewish love poem, of all things—at last we find mention of the magic name. Although the *Mishna*, or written traditions of the Jews, refer to Jesus several times, his name is never associated with any town. The Old Testament has never heard of the place nor is there a single reference to it in the 22,000 words of St. Paul's Epistles although, naturally, there is extensive mention of Jesus. As the Epis-

24

tles were written some twenty-five years before the first
gospel appeared, their failure to mention 'Nazareth' might
be significant. It is only fair to observe that neither do
they associate Jesus with any other town.

The most curious silence, however—and perhaps the
most ominous—is that of Josephus, the garrulous Jewish
historian of the 1st century. More than an historian, he
was also a priest of the Temple and, on his mother's side,
a descendant of the very Hasmonean kings whose throne,
we say, Jesus endeavoured to restore, and as a result paid
the usual penalty for treason.

Josephus tells us that the four chief sects of the Jews
were the Pharisees, Sadducees, Essenes and Zealots, and
that he had been a member of all three of the first-named
at various times. As we know that the Zealots were fanatical Hasmonean royalists intent on the restoration, we are
inclined to think that his membership of the Hasmonean
clan makes suspect his implied denial ever to have been
also a Zealot.

Suspicion turns to downright certainty when we discover that, on the outbreak of the fatal war with Rome in
66 A.D., Josephus was made Commander-in-Chief of the
vital Galilee area, which was not only where the Romans
were rightly expected to strike first but contained the
Zealot's nest of Kana and, above it on Mount Hasmon,
their eyrie and fortress of Jotapata, ever to be associated
with the treacherous Josephus.

It is impossible to believe that he owed his military appointment to anything else but the fact that he was a
prominent Hasmonean and Zealot.

His first task was to raise an army of the tough
Galileans and his second, to fortify all cities that were
strategically important. As every commander in history
who ever campaigned in Galilee has admitted, no defence
of the province is possible without control of the range of
hills squatting in its very centre. From the topmost height,
the flat land revealed troop movements vast distances
away, while the range itself provided a short cut from the
classic battlegrounds of the Plain of Netofa to the north
to that of Esdraelon to the south. Truly, whoever held
that topmost hill controlled all Galilee. And if we are to
believe the gospels, sitting on a spur two hundred feet
from the top of that hill, was Nazareth. But was it there
in Jesus' time?

Josephus fortified about a dozen of Galilee's most strategically important cities ... and names them. Yet he doesn't so much as mention the most important of them all. Why? Was it because Nazareth didn't need fortifying? Few would agree. Was it already fortified? No traces are visible. Sprawled as it is along that spur, if defence were its function then present Nazareth was sited by a military fool for it is dominated by that higher hill, amazingly left vacant for any invader to occupy at his leisure. But was it vacant?

The author of *Luke* calls Nazareth a 'city'—using the Greek word *'polis'* which the present place certainly was not until comparatively recent times. If ancient Nazareth were not a *'polis'* why did the author deliberately select this word to describe it when he had a range of definitive others to classify it accurately?

Remarkably enough, there are unmistakable signs that a *'polis'* must once have stood on the topmost peak, though it is unlikely that its name was ever Nazareth. Had it been, Josephus would certainly have listed it; he reports several skirmishes in the immediate vicinity of present Nazareth but never so much as once mentions its name.

However—and here's a very odd thing—he makes frequent mention of Galilee's state capital, Sepphoris, which frequently played an important role in the Zealot's operations, but is never once mentioned in any of the four gospels. Why? is a very good question. Did Jesus never visit the place where Judas the Galilean—probably a relative—scored a triumph by raiding the capital's armoury to equip his followers? Judas was crucified for his crime and the fuming Romans burned Sepphoris to the ground, after killing the citizens for their treachery, of course. It is strange if Jesus never visited this glittering place, because it was scarcely five miles from present Nazareth, and downhill all the way. Perhaps the explanation is that, like Nazareth, the city of Sepphoris didn't exist in Jesus' day.

If we are to believe the guidebooks, Sepphoris always stood where its tumbled ruins presently lie, in the lower foothills about five miles north of Nazareth, but that this was always so is to be doubted.

The present Sepphoris ruins consist of nothing more than a few tumbled stones no more than about eight hundred years old, yet it is certain that an extensive and beautiful city once stood here, within a complex of Graeco-Roman style public buildings, elaborate villas, amphitheatres, aqueducts and so on. We know that it was once known as Diocaesarea because the Emperor Antonius Pius so named it in the 2nd century. The question to be asked is whether that was a new name bestowed on the old city of Sepphoris or on a completely new and different city?

Josephus described Sepphoris' defences as 'impregnable'; they could never have justified this description, no matter how impossibly tall or thick its walls. However, had Sepphoris been the name of the city that once stood on the hill above Nazareth, even light fortifications might well have entitled it to consider itself impregnable.

Although an Israeli archaeologist, Mr. Itzchak Sheynis, said to be expert on the present ruins, is inclined to disagree, there seems no good reason why Sepphoris on-the-hill—after its destruction by the Romans—might not have been decreed to lie in ruins for ever after as a punishment for its assistance to Judas the Galilean Zealot. This sort of thing was nothing new; ancient Carthage was not only destroyed but, after its stones were carted off to serve elsewhere, the site was cross-ploughed then strewn with a heavy dressing of salt so that nothing would ever grow there again. Roman desolation of cities was no novelty to the Jews.

Possibly, after Sepphoris on-the-hill had lain a desolate, blackened ruin for a number of years, a few survivors from the massacre of its former citizens crept back to the area. Forbidden ever again to occupy the hill, they might have commenced a new settlement which, eventually, became Nazareth. When this is likely to have happened—if it happened—it is impossible to say, but an educated guess would be sometime during the 2nd century when the influx of Roman colonists displaced and dispossessed the Jews and turned Judea into an almost completely Roman colony.

If we assume that the survivors of the Sepphoris massacre had settled five miles downhill to the north and had built a humble new Sepphoris where the present ruins lie, they would have been booted out when the Roman colonists arrived. Forced to seek a new home once more, what is more likely than that their descendants had trekked uphill and established the settlement called Nazareth? The Sepphoris taken over by the Romans would then have been expanded and elaborated and, as it was, renamed Diocaesarea.

However the way of it really was, the suspicion that the city which had once stood on the hill was, indeed, the original Sepphoris, was strengthened about a century ago by the discovery of an odd stone plaque in the vicinity of Nazareth. Chiselled into its face in *koine* (common) Greek—read and spoken by most Jews at that time—was an Imperial Decree, probably of Caesar Augustus, who died in 14 A.D. The plaque warned that those who damaged tombs, exhumed the dead, transferred bodies from one tomb to another or who defaced or removed inscriptions or other parts of a sepulchre, committed an heinous crime against the *gods* (note the fascinating polytheistic plural) and that for these crimes, but particularly for changing the place of a body's burial, the penalty was death!

As the plaque almost certainly pre-dated the birth of Jesus it could not have referred to the most famous empty tomb of all, as so many Christians hopefully thought. Obviously, it was merely a general warning against a crime which was growing too prevalent to please either the Roman overlords . . . or their thirty thousand gods.

Where, it is reasonable to ask, would such a general warning plaque have been displayed? Far too expensive to permit a separate sign to be issued to every village in Judea, is it not likely that one was put up in the capital of every state or province where, presumably, the most people would see it and would gossip about it to those who did not? The most likely place, then, for its display in Galilee would have been in the marketplace of Sepphoris.

The fact that it was found where it was is due, one suggests, to nothing else but that this is where it landed when tossed down the hill by the Roman troops wrecking the original capital city of Sepphoris. Crashing down the hill, it finally came to rest 'in the vicinity of Nazareth'.

One final—and telling—piece of evidence against the claim that, historically, Jesus was known as 'Jesus of Nazareth' is also provided by Josephus. In what is known as the Slavonic Version or Edition of 'The Jewish War', there are found strange sections—not present in any other edition or in the original—dealing with John the Baptist, Jesus and the Crucifixion, and a few other matters of interest to Christians. Totalling somewhere about one thousand five hundred words, they stand suspect by many scholars as being bogus additions designed to get Jesus into the history books. Whatever might be the truth of the matter, the strange thing about the passages is that the name Jesus is mentioned only twice, and on no occasion is he called 'Jesus of Nazareth'; in fact, the longest passage of all about him doesn't even mention his name. In one very curious brief comment, whoever it was wrote the insert refers to him as 'Jesus, the King who never reigned!'

The relevant thing about these passages—true or bogus—is that whether they were the work of Josephus or of enthusiastic Christians, the truth would seem to be that 'Christ', historically, was not known as Jesus of Nazareth. While this doesn't entitle the conclusion that he was known as 'Jesus of Gennesareth' at least the possibility remains that he might have been.

4 / A Scandal in the Family

Amid the shrill screams of the devout, most objective New Testament scholars today dismiss the gospel accounts of the conception, birth and lineage of Jesus as a mixture of contrived fictions and demonstrable myths in which, like the needle in the haystack, might be hidden one tiny grain of truth representing an actual historical event. They point to a dozen pagan cults containing so many elements common to the fanciful tales surrounding the generation of Jesus, that only the most bigoted can have minds utterly free of suspicion.

The Indian legend of the birth of Krishna the Redeemer, for example, relates how his coming was annunciated to the virgin, Jasoda, who was destined to be his mother. Following this news, Vishnu the sun god assumed bodily form and got the virgin with child. At his birth, the shepherds came to adore while the jealous rajahs ordered that every male child born on the same night as Krishna should be killed.

The myth's parallelism with the Christian fantasy is so remarkable that, if no plagiarism were involved, this must surely be one of the best recorded cases in history in which truth was, indeed, stranger than fiction.

Although St. Paul predeceased the arrival of even the very first gospel to publish the nonsense, it is clear that wild tales were flying around the inns and marketplaces of Judea from an early date, and that he took firm steps to deal with them. Unequivocally he wrote: 'Jesus was born according to the flesh!', which not only means what it bluntly says, but leaves no room for the absurd gossip that 'God did it!' As to the rest, he disposed of them by writing: '. . . neither give heed to fables and to endless genealogies!' His advice went unheeded by the authors of *Matthew* and *Luke*—or their editors—with the result that what started out as a typical example of Oriental exaggeration and gossip was foisted on to the credulous world of paganism and, by inheritance, on to the no less credulous world of Christianity, even into the 20th century.

In the early Church's deliberate use of these absurd fantasies we can see, perhaps, the first stirrings of a primitive Madison Avenue. It is no accident that the only two gospels to carry them were those clearly intended for the edification of the pagans. The Church undoubtedly reasoned that if Christianity were to succeed in the world outside Judea—having failed inside—it would have to be presented to the pagans in terms and symbols which they were familiar with and understood. Jesus had to be given a genesis and background of unparalleled prestige sufficient to outrank any pagan deity, and it was all rolled into a slick package which came in two sizes—*Matthew* and *Luke*—not only with the guarantee of eternal life, but with the proud claim, 'Our God is better than your god!' It was, in short, a kind of theological 'whiter-than-white' campaign.

This was tacitly admitted by Jerome—the 4th century theologian and producer of the Vulgate—who saw the superstitious legend of Jesus' birth as no more than that 'such as all founders of religions and heroes had'.

The campaign succeeded for its seeds were sown in the fertile soil of superstition. The pagans were long familiar with the ability of randy gods to swoop on human maidens and set their eyes afire. As an example of what Christianity had to beat—and it wasn't much—here is an historical example.

When the mother of the future Alexander the Great discovered the embarrassing consequences of a night of mad, gay, frolic she convinced her furious husband, Phillip of Macedon, that the great god Jupiter Ammon had 'kindled the fire in her belly'. Instantly his rage vanished, to be replaced by awe that his wife had been so honoured. When the child was born, the plain cuckold proudly presented him to the court as his own 'god-given' son and heir. The subsequent military genius of the child who grew up to conquer half the then-known world before he was thirty, suggests that the great god Jupiter must have crept into the lady's bed-chamber disguised as one of Phillip of Macedon's more brilliant Generals . . . or vice-versa.

The very same expediency which had demanded that Jesus should have been generated by God also turned his

mother into a goddess. Hyperdulia, or the worship of the
Virgin Mary—also called Marianity or Mariology—owes
its origin to the fact that the most popular Roman goddess
which Christianity had to combat was Isis, the former
Egyptian deity whose son had also been generated by a
god. Isis worship could be countered only by the new faith
absorbing the pagan goddess, and so Isis became Mary the
Mother of God, even assuming the pagan deity's titles of
'Redemptress' and 'Star of the Sea'. In fact, the very first
statues of Mary in Rome were merely those of Isis
with—literally—a new coat of paint; even her elaborate
temples were taken over to house the chief goddess of the
new paganism.

For the first three centuries the Church had ignored
Mary, but after the Roman Empire had fallen to Christianity and Constantine's Council of Nicea had conducted
its extraordinary ballot of the Bishops—which decided
that Jesus was Divine, the Son of God and God himself—
it became obvious that some special status was required
for his mother.

The wheels of hyperdulia began turning with the astonishing proposal of Chrysostom, the 4th century Patriarch
of Constantinople, that Mary had experienced 'perpetual
virginity'. Put bluntly, he argued that Mary's hymen had
remained intact not only through the process of conception, but was still so after the birth of Jesus. Even more
remarkably—if that is possible—the thesis of virginity was
extended to the very end of her earthly life. The fact that
Mary had other sons and daughters after her first-born
was neatly sidestepped by the claim that these were not
Jesus' natural brothers and sisters, but cousins.

Naturally enough, Chrysostom's proposals ran into violent trouble and opposition, for not all in the Church were
bereft of their reason. At the same time, Chrysostom had
some supporters he could well have done without; for instance, Ephraem Syrus who argued that Mary had been
impregnated auricularly: 'It entered through the ear and
hid itself in her womb.' Ingenious—or ingenuous—though
this was, while it might have solved the problem of im-
pregnation for the 4th century Church, it still left unsolved
the problem of Jesus' miraculous birth. Not to be considered seriously, the Syrus solution is mentioned not merely
to indicate both the ignorance and credulity of the times,
but the absurd lengths to which some in the Church—

seemingly more psychotic than saintly—were prepared to go in the cause of evolving doctrine. However, if it comes to the point, there was nothing that could have been said about Syrus' crazy solution that could not have been said twice as strongly about Chrysostom's.

The strange thing is that it seems never to have occurred to anyone that they were trying to find answers to a question equally absurd as: How many angles has a four-sided triangle? The old rule about a logical, but absurd, answer requiring that the criteria be re-checked, still holds good. In the event, doctrine had passed the point of no return; the error had been made and could never be un-made; all that could be done was talk fast and bore straight for the guns. So one step up the ladder of non-sense led to another.

When, in 431, the Council of Ephesus proclaimed Mary *Deipara* or Mother of God, the way was paved for the success of John Chrysostom's amazing 'perpetual virginity' solution which the Lateran Council made dogma some two hundred and fifty years later.

For the next seven centuries the ecclesiastical brains-trust had too much on its plate of an earthly nature to worry over-much with the status of its gods. There were heretics to burn and riches to be got, wars to be fought, documents to be forged and the Church taken out of the heady heights of Heaven into the real world of political intrigue and power. Mention Charlemagne, and the Church blushes; whisper a word of the False Decretals, and it goes red in the face. Still, in the monasteries of Christendom were men who, if they had forgotten Jesus, had not forgotten his Mother.

The time had clearly come for Mary to be elevated a little further by proclaiming her free of all sin which, historically, she was not. In 1546 the Council of Trent asserted that she was and, by so doing, gave birth to the doctrine of Immaculate Conception which, three centuries later, Pope Pius IX promoted to become an Article of Faith. At once, Christianity blasted off from the pad of reason—where it had been wobbling uncertainly for 1800 years—and sped far out into the black night spaces of sheer theophilosophical madness. It has not been sighted since!

Now the pace of Mary's glorification rapidly increased. At the Mariological Congress at Lourdes in 1958, it was daringly proposed that she be proclaimed *causa effi-ciens*—the agent or cause that produces—of Redemption without whose intercession and mediation no grace could fall from God above on to the faithful below. It failed, but only temporarily.

In 1964—the very year that the 'fifteenth scroll' emerged in Israel—Pope Paul VI elevated Mary to *Mater Ecclesiae* (Mother of the Church) and, automatically, she became *causa efficiens;* from that moment, Roman Catholics could speak to God only through the Redemptress, and so were in much the same position as the unfortunate Cabots of Boston.

It should be added that Pope Paul's decision was both wilful and almost solitary, for His Holiness made it in the face of the almost total opposition of Vatican Council 2 which, reasonably enough, saw little hope of any real ecumenism with the dissident sects of Protestantism if Mary were further glorified. Pope Paul VI however—like all popes since 1870—enjoys an infallibility not granted by the Church to that earlier Paul, the architect of Christianity, and so he won the day. Mary was now, as *Mater Ecclesiae*, the very co-equal of God. Isis the Redemptress had come a long way.

Now the images of the Holy Virgin in the tens of thousands of Catholic Churches throughout Christendom blazed with a new and glorious splendour while Jesus, her son, hung in agony on the walls, almost forgotten.

Though it might not have been what the Church intended—though it should have forseen—there is little doubt that from the frequency and intensity with which they are prayed to and adored, the images of the new Marianity constitute the very same pagan idolatry which Christianity was supposed to replace and transcend. St. Paul, it seems, was wrong in asserting that Jesus emerged from the tomb; what really came out was the Church, which seems bent on changing its faith from Christian to Marian as swiftly as it can. And the tragic thing is, that it has all been due to a scribe's error!

5 / The Faith's First Divorce

Was the historical Mary, the Mother of Jesus, a virgin during his conception? The answer must be 'yes, she wasn't'.

If, by 'virgin' is meant *'virgo intacta'*—now rapidly becoming both rare and obsolescent—then Mary failed to qualify. Despite this, however, she was still a virgin within the strict definition of Judaism, and it is in the apparent contradiction that all the confusion originally arose.

The matter would not be canvassed at all but for the necessity to endeavour to check the claim by Jesus of Gennesareth—author of the 'fifteenth scroll'—that his father had been named *Ya'akob* or Jacob. If the scroll author were, in fact, the historical Jesus—whose story, in part, provided the basis of the gospels—then we should expect to find either some evidence of the fact or of its concealment, in the gospels. Additionally, we might expect to find a possible clue to Jesus' father in the identity of the man who later fathered Mary's many other children. In order to do this, this absurd dispute of her 'virginity' must first be disposed of.

Put as simply as possible, the confusion arose because Ptolemy Philadelphus of Egypt, somewhere about 270 B.C., had the Hebrew Old Testament translated into Greek for the benefit of the large Jewish population of Alexandria who no longer spoke or read Hebrew. The result was the famous Septuagint, so-called either because some seventy scholars participated in its translation or because the work took only seventy days from start to finish.

When they came to *Isaiah* 7:14, they struck quite a problem. The verse reads: 'Behold, a virgin shall conceive and bear a son, and shall call his name Immanuel.' Now the passage, with the three verses following is entirely symbolical and was intended as a prophecy of what was to happen to Israel.

However, the verse still had to be translated and the difficulty was that Greek had only one word for 'virgin', which was 'parthenos' and uncompromisingly meant what it said, a physical virgin who had had no sexual experience and whose hymen was intact. Hebrew, on the other hand, had two, 'almah' and 'bethulah', because their life style considered that retention of virginity once a girl reached the age of marriage—usually fourteen—was a disgrace and an insult to God. Now, while the Hebrew word 'bethulah' exactly translated into its Greek counterpart 'parthenos', the catch was that the scripture used the Hebrew word 'almah' which meant a 'young, unmarried woman' or, possibly more correctly, a woman of any age, married or not, whose womb had not produced fruit. There being no Greek equivalent for 'almah', the scholars either had to leave a blank or write the word 'parthenos'—which is what they did.

When the gospels came to be written centuries later, the author of *Matthew* thumbed a copy of the Greek Septuagint seeking prophecies from the past which might support the truth of the rumours about the mysterious birth of Jesus, particularly that he had been generated by God.

Being a Greek and writing in Greek, it was only natural that when he came to *Isaiah* 7:14 and struck the word 'parthenos', he should have read it quite literally . . . and with superstitious amazement. What wonder was this foretold in the ancient Scriptures? A *virgin* bear a child? Then the gossip was true!

In just such a way, then, was probably sown the seed of the Immaculate Conception myth. After *Matthew* came *Luke* whose author—also a non-Jew—would also have had to use the Greek Septuagint and, meeting the word 'parthenos', would have been able to come to no other conclusion than had *Matthew*. It is altogether significant that neither of the two *Jewish* gospel authors—*Mark* and *John* repeated the folly because, having access to the Hebrew Scriptures, they would have read the original word 'almah' and, seeing nothing unusual in a young unmarried woman bearing a child, would have flipped the page and passed on.

The matter has been explored at greater length than is usual because it is high time that it was; too often the reader is confronted by an *opinion* which presents insufficient supporting evidence to enable him to form his own.

One may please himself whether he dismisses the birth anecdotes as myth, error or the echo of some actual historical event embellished with a wealth of highly imaginative detail for the benefit of the pagans.

The proven fact that many scurrilous stories were circulating about Jesus' parentage during the 1st century certainly points to some doubt about the matter and suggests that Mary was involved in something of a scandal. *Matthew* and *Luke* extricate her from this with their claim that 'God did it!' but, as we have seen, this was only to explain the utter impossibility of a *virgin* bearing a child unless God had been the father. Having cleared up their error, we are left with the possibly historical grain of truth that this was the actual situation: a young, unmarried woman, betrothed to a man called Joseph, was found to be with child.

As it is certain that Joseph wasn't responsible, it is equally certain that some other man was.

The marriage customs and sexual mores of the Hebrews are too complex to be discussed at length here; suffice to say that retention of virginity beyond the normal age for marriage—14 for girls and eighteen for men—was considered to be a sin against God, and barrenness a curse. The act of marriage was separated into two significant parts, the *'qiddushin'* or betrothal, and the *'nissu'in'*, which was the actual wedding, which generally took place within a year of the betrothal.

Although it is uncertain whether or not 1st century Judaism permitted betrothed couples to have sexual intercourse, this had certainly been the custom in the past and it might still have been so in isolated or conservative parts of the country, or even in families. However that might have been, although the custom might seem to us to be both permissive and even immoral, the whole point about it was the getting of children as speedily as possible. These might even be born before the actual wedding—as the gospels report Jesus was—but still were considered legitimate. In fact, so binding was the betrothal that any girl who had intercourse with a strange man was guilty of adultery, and was at once liable to the penalty such a sin required. There is argument as to whether or not this still included stoning to death. Perhaps it did. Certainly this is indicated by the gospel tale of the woman taken in adultery: 'He that is without sin among you, let him first cast

a stone at her.' However, as this is considered to have
been introduced into the gospel of *John* only in the 4th
century, it cannot be relied upon.

When Mary broke the news of her condition to Joseph
he was both ashamed and furious, reminding us a little of
Phillip of Macedon in similar circumstances and who was
given the identical 'God did it!' explanation used by Mary.
Joseph found himself on the horns of a dilemma.

We are told, by inference, that he still loved his way-
ward betrothed for, as *Matthew* says: 'Then Joseph her
"husband", being a just man, and not willing to make her
a public example ...' What this passage means is that he
was unwilling to publicly accuse her of adultery which, if
proved, would have led to at least her social ostracism, if
nothing worse.

Recoiling from this, he determined to 'put her away
privily', which means that he would put her out of his life
by what was known as a *'git'* or *'gittin'* or a secret Bill of
Divorcement. Under such a document—which was privately witnessed—the divorced couple merely went their
ways and no filing of the *'git'* was required by the authorities concerned. Though it might guess a lot, the public
never knew for certain what had happened and the guilty
party—particularly the woman—was spared the humilia-
tion of a washing of her affairs in public. More important,
the law of Judaism demanded no penalty.

Deciding to sleep on the problem, Joseph had a
dream—so we are told—in which an angel of the Lord
appeared and confirmed Mary's explanation of her condition with the news: 'that which is conceived in her is of
the Holy Ghost'. Then, according to *Matthew*: 'Joseph did
as the angel of the Lord had bidden and took unto himself
his wife.'

This can only mean that he forgave Mary and con-
doned her crime—for crime it was in the eyes of the
Law—which is historically wrong because it was absolutely impossible for a Jew of those times to have done
such a thing!

The Law of the *Mishna* provided three counts on any
one of which a man was *compelled* to divorce his wife:
adultery, clandestine or secret intercourse, and leprosy,
which probably meant, by that time, any form of venereal
disease rather than the classic leprosy of the Old Testament. The Law was very strict and its penalties for eva-

sion, severe. Expressly prohibited was the slightest condonation of adultery, yet we are asked to believe that this is precisely what Joseph—a devout Jew—actually did. Which is nonsense!

Stressing that the one thing which a man in his position must *not* do was *nothing,* and that he had to take positive action—which must be prompt and in accord with the Law—the *Mishna* provided Joseph with only two options; he could denounce Mary as an adulteress or he could divorce her—whether publicly or privately was up to him—but it had to be one thing or the other . . . and fast!

As he neither denounced nor publicly divorced her, and as even the gospel affirms that he had decided on a private divorce until his dream of the angel, we can only assume that, historically, this is what he actually did. So it seems likely that Mary was the first divorcee in the religion's history.

Significantly, it is precisely at this point that Joseph vanished from the story, with the exception of two dubious incidents whose authenticity is open to some doubt. These are, Joseph at Jesus' circumcision—inserted to allow Simeon to recognise the Christ—and the 12 year old Jesus lecturing in the Temple. This episode occurs only in *Luke* and almost parallels an incident which the historian Josephus relates about himself. As tradition has had vague hints about the possible connection between Josephus and the author of *Luke,* it is both odd to meet with the tale in the gospel and to discover—in Paul's Epistle to the Phillipians 2:25—a scribe who bore the name of Epaphroditus, which also happened to be exactly the same as that of the publisher of the works of Flavius Josephus. While they might have been two quite separate men, the intriguing possibility exists that they were not. If so, the possibilities are such that we had better leave them unexplored.

After the secret Bill of Divorcement was signed, it seems reasonable to assume—from his absence from events—that Joseph had either died or, much more likely, had proceeded to put as much distance as possible between him and the object of his unfortunate affections. Whatever the reason, he vanished. Left alone, what is Mary likely to have done?

The *'git'* signed by both parties provided—and twice emphasised—that the guilty party became free to remarry the moment the witnesses had appended their signatures. To quote the operative phrase as it applied to Mary: '... any man whom thou desirest.' Being with child, isn't it probably that she would have turned to the man responsible? It is suggested that this is precisely what she did!

Although it will come as no surprise to any New Testament scholar, it will astonish those Christians unaware of the early traditions the Holy Family engendered or the battles-royal fought over them by the various factions supporting this tale or that, that the man whom Mary married immediately after her divorce can be identified ... because he is named in the gospels!

The same Eusebius who is called 'The Father of Ecclesiastical History'—probably justly, because he was the man who produced those fifty new copies of the gospels for Constantine—tells a curious tale, which there is no reason to doubt.

Eusebius writes that according to an even earlier church historian named Hegesippus—who lived in Jerusalem and was a Jew—Joseph had a brother whose name was either Clophas or Cleophas. When these names are examined they prove to derive from the Armaic '*Halphi*' which, in turn, we discover to be another form of the name, Alpheus.

And Alpheus, it might be recalled, is named in the gospels as the *father* of Jesus' brothers and sisters!

6 / Jesus' Real Father

There must have been many times when Christianity had wished that certain parts of the New Testament either had never been written or had suffered at the hands of perceptive editors; or even, still being with us, that they would self destruct in the standard five seconds. Among these, none can have been more the object of its wishful thinking than those embarrassing passages which refer to Jesus' brothers and sisters.

Having maintained for 1300 years the doctrine of Mary's perpetual virginity—expressed as *ante partum, in partu, post partum,* or that before, during and after Jesus' birth Mary was a virgin—it has endeavoured to sweep under the carpet the fact that Jesus had siblings by the pretence that 'brethren' and 'brothers' actually meant cousins.

While it is true that the Hebrew *'akim'* was often applied to both, the fact that it *was* applied to both does not justify the stand that it was only applied to cousins. Further, to suggest that the 1st century Jew had no verbal means of distinguishing between these two important elements of the tribe or family—in a land where the Laws of Inheritance were vital to society—is to play very loosely with the facts.

Peculiarly enough, the faith's strange interpretation is not applied to *Luke* 3:1 in which Herod's brother Philip is mentioned. Should we disregard the known facts of history and believe that Philip was Herod's cousin? Are we to misread the gospels and believe that Elizabeth and Mary were not cousins but sisters? Were the disciples, Peter and Andrew, cousins instead of brothers? Is the same argument to be used to transform the other brothers, John and James Zebedee, into each other's cousin?

Whatever merit there might be concerning the ambiguity of the Hebrew *'akim'*, none would deny that no room for confusion exists in Greek. Let us skip over the fact that the first three gospels were, by modern opinion, all written in Greek and that whatever 'akim' might have meant is not relevant; let us turn away temporarily from the gospel evidence to the earliest known witness to the existence of at least one brother of Jesus, St. Paul.

In *Galatians* 1:18-19 he wrote: 'Then after three years I went up to Jerusalem to see Peter, and abode with him fifteen days. But of the other apostles saw I none, save *James the Lord's Brother*.'

Paul was writing in Greek, which has separate words for 'brother' and 'cousin', and yet wrote 'brother'. Was he lying, or mistaken?

This same James, the Lord's brother, is also described in the gospels as the son of Alpheus, as are several others who, therefore, must also be regarded as Jesus' brothers. As brothers require a common father and Alpheus is James', then he is also father of Jesus.

Quintus Septimus Florens Tertullian was a notable 'Father of the Church' whose life straddled both the 2nd and 3rd centuries. Was he misinformed or misguided when, in a dispute which almost tore the Church apart, he stoutly maintained that the Lord's brethren were 'Jesus' uterine brothers'? Hell-bent on proving the continuing virginity of Mary, his opponents used every speculative distortion possible to deny the evidence right before their eyes in the gospels. Most of it is still there for anyone to read today, although how it survived the perilous 4th century when so much 'editorialising' appears to have taken place, perhaps only God knows! Wrong or right, old Q. S. F. Tertullian might have been far more on the ball of the historical facts than the proponents of the sentimental, supernatural and medically-miraculous doctrine that eventually swept him away.

So what are the facts? The earliest evidence of all has been presented—St. Paul's—so now we turn to the gospels and *Matthew* 1:25: 'And he (Joseph) knew her (Mary) not until she had brought forth her first-born son ...' As the very earliest gospel commentators have noted, the implications inherent in the phrase 'her first-born son' are that there was a 'second-born' son at some later date. Other gospel evidence supports this; for example, the celebrated family roll call in *Matthew* 13:55-56: 'Is this not the carpenter's son? Is not his mother called Mary? And his brethren, James and Joses and Simon and Judas? And his sisters, are they not all with us?'

According to that list Jesus had four brothers and at least two sisters, possibly more.

A significantly different rendition is given by the parallel passage in *Mark* 6:3: 'Is this not the carpenter, the brother of James, and Joses, and of Judas, and Simon? And are not his sisters here with us?' That would seem to be explicit enough for all but the most disputatious. It will be noted that *Mark* calls Jesus a carpenter, while *Matthew* describes him as the *son* of a carpenter. It is this difference that is significant and which enables us to point to another glaring example of textual manipulation of the gospels.

Before passing to it, however, it is not without interest to mention that as in the case of the Wise Men who came to adore the infant Jesus—whom the gospels nowhere describe as three in number—there is no instance of Joseph ever being called a carpenter. All that *Matthew* says is that Jesus was the *son* of one, which is not quite the same thing as saying that Joseph was a carpenter. According to the traditionally accepted tale, Joseph wasn't Jesus' father at all; Jesus was the son of God and as we can't quite see God with an adze in his hands, the carpenter reference must be to Jesus' real male parent, Alpheus.

The famous 3rd century theologian, Origen, was probably the first of the Ecclesiastical Establishment to draw attention to editorial manipulation of the gospels. Evidently there had arisen some oral tradition that Jesus had followed his real father's trade and Origen wanted to put it down. He tried to do this by drawing attention to the fact that nowhere in the gospels did he find the slightest suggestion that Jesus had been a carpenter, yet here is the explicit *Mark* 6:3 staring us in the face. As it had not been there in Origen's day, because he complained that it was not to be found in any of the gospels used in the Christian *churches*, obviously it was added at some subsequent date. The only reason that can be seen for such an apparently minor insertion is the need to draw attention away from the carpenter father, which reinforces the suspicion that it had been Alpheus and not Joseph who had really plied the saw and the hammer.

Maintenance of the doctrinal fiction that Mary did not re-marry has led the Church into a maze-like jungle from which it can never escape as long as the gospels provide abundant evidence to the contrary, and identify her husband as Alpheus.

Not even the Church disputes that Alpheus had a wife named Mary, by whom he had several children who are frankly called Jesus' brothers. What it bitterly disputes is that they were his *brothers*. It does this by the sickening defence that Alpheus' wife Mary was the *sister* of the Virgin. Two daughters with the same name in a family? How confusing! How unlikely! As far as we know for certain, the Virgin Mary had only one sister, who was Salome, the mother of two of Jesus' disciples, James and John Zebedee.

This is the same Salome who, according to *Matthew* and *Mark*, was one of the small group of women who stood by the Cross at the Crucifixion. Both gospel authors agree that there were three in the group: Mary Magdalene, and Mary the mother of James and of Joses, and the mother of Zebedee's children (Salome). While *Luke* mentions a group of women, he fails to identify any of its members. However, if Mary the mother of James and Joses is not to be identified in the named groups as also the Mother of Jesus, then we can only come to the conclusion that the Holy Mother did not attend the Crucifixion ... when the gospel of *John*, whose author was an eyewitness, says that she did. And it is here, in *John*, that the cat really pops out of the bag.

According to *John* 19:25: 'Now there stood by the cross of Jesus his mother, and his mother's sister, Mary the wife of Cleophas (Alpheus), and Mary Magdalene.'

The Church, of course, uses this verse as 'proof' that Mary had a sister Mary, which is nonsense. Either that verse refers to four women—the Virgin and her sister and Mary wife of Alpheus and Mary Magdalene—or it refers to three and, to this extent, harmonises with *Matthew* and *Mark*. If four, then the Virgin's sister is quite distinct from Mary wife of Alpheus; if three, then—it being impossible for there to have been two Mary's in the family—it must be assumed that the phrase 'and his mother's sister' has been misplaced and was so done in order to conceal the embarrassing truth of an eyewitness's revelation.

Rearranged in the way in which it must originally have

stood, it would read 'Now there stood by the cross of
Jesus his mother Mary the wife of Alpheus, and his
mother's sister (Salome), and Mary Magdalene.'

Now everything falls into place and the list of three
now exactly tallies with those of the other two gospel authors, *Matthew* and *Mark*. As the list in *John* presently
stands it is impossibly incorrect, for which the gospel-au-
thor eyewitness cannot be held responsible. He saw what
he saw and reported it but, clearly, this didn't suit the requirements of the 4th century theology which had already
gone overboard for Mary's Perpetual Virginity which, of
course, demanded that—whatever the historical facts
might have been—she had no husband and no children
subsequent to Jesus.

As our sole interest in the subject lies in the extent to
which the gospel evidence might be found to support the
claim of Jesus of Gennesareth, author of the 'fifteenth
scroll', that his father had been named *Ya'akob* or Jacob,
we have endeavoured to show that there was more than
reasonable doubt that the father of Jesus was either
Joseph or God but was, in fact, a man called Alpheus.
How far, then, does Alpheus really help our search?

In the 1st century A.D. it was common practice for
male Jews to adopt a fashionable Greek name for public
use, retaining their given Hebrew name for use by family
or intimates. A typical example was Simon called Petros.
Although it is not evident in the case of Petros or Peter,
as far as possible a man taking a Greek alternative name
endeavoured to choose one with the same meaning; this
being a factor of great importance to Jews.

Although it is impossible to say so with any certainty, it
is possible that the meaning of Alpheus (successor) might
lead us to the man's given Jewish name by discovering
which one had the same or a very similar meaning. As Alpheus, we say, replaced Mary's betrothed husband, Joseph,
he was well named for he certainly was a successor so it is
with little surprise that we discover that the Jewish name
which also bore this meaning was ... *Ya'akob* or Jacob,
which just happened to be the name of the father of Jesus
of Gennesareth ... as it was, we say, of Jesus of Nazareth.

Are we coming closer, perhaps, to the possibility—once
considered remote—that the bogus 'Professor Grosset'

7 / The Original Sign of the Cross

The brilliant tragic saga of the Maccabees began with the flourish of a bloody, sacrificial meatcleaver one day in 166 B.C., and ended only in 135 A.D. with the defeat and death of the known last of them, Simon ben Kosebah, 'Son of the Star', Prince of Israel, Messiah!

Between their curtain's rise and fall were exactly 300 years of glory, riches, murder, usurpation and persecution, during which their descendants were hunted down like rats and, one by one, exterminated, however long that took.

Strictly speaking, there was no such family as the Maccabees; this was purely the personal 'nom-de-guerre' of Judas ben Mattathias, who was known as the Lord's or God's 'Hammer' because he wore a device or symbol shaped like this ancient tool—called in the Hebrew 'makkabah'—and smote God's enemies in smashing, hammer-like blows.

And the device?

Would you believe a Cross?

Embarrassing though it will be to those Christians who imagine—because they have been so told—that everything associated with their faith originated in the glorious tragedy of Jesus of Nazareth, the fact is that Judas Maccabeus probably marched into battle under the protection of the Cross!

It will be recalled that the night before the Exodus of the ancient Jews from Egypt, the faithful were instructed to protect themselves from the Angel of Death who would 'pass over' the city that night by making a secret sign on their doors with blood. Reason suggests that the sign must have been one known only to the Hebrews, could be boldly and hurriedly drawn and couldn't be mistaken for anything but what it was by the assassins who—in the guise of Angels of Death—that night slew the occupants of every house not bearing the secret mark.

47

In those times, the Hebrews used the Canaanite or Phoenician alphabet, for the square Aramaic letters of modern Hebrew still lay in the future. It is thought that the letter symbol most likely to have been chosen as the secret sign was 'tau', which was then shaped like a cross.

That this speculation is correct is indicated by *Ezekiel* 9:4, which applies to events eight hundred years after the Exodus:

> And the Lord said unto him, go through the midst of Jerusalem, and set a mark upon the foreheads of the men that sigh and that cry for all the abominations that be done in the midst thereof.

In the Latin edition of the Scriptures known as the Vulgate, it is specifically stated that the sign to be used *is* the letter 'tau', which makes it that much more likely that this was the same sign used in the Exodus episode. As, in both stories, the faithful escaped the slaughter that followed, one makes the startling suggestion that what was actually 'the sign of the cross' was a 'charm' connected with the saving from physical harm and death many centuries before the Crucifixion, from which it is claimed to have derived.

It is surely but a small step in primitive religious philosophy to extend the magic sign's protection of the physical body to the spiritual soul, thus promising eternal life.

Until comparatively recently and, perhaps, to this very day, a strange group of itinerant smiths and carpenters known as the Sleb—who lead the Bedouin life in Syria—owe their name to the fact that they wear the mark of a cross on their foreheads. This, surely, is *Ezekiel* 9:4 before our very eyes. Apart from the fascinating possibility that the Sleb might have derived from a fleeing remnant of the Maccabees, their wearing of the cross requires that we have a long look at Jesus' warning that those eager to follow him 'must each bear his cross'. Though this has been interpreted as an allusion to the Cross of Calvary it might well have meant that each must literally bear such a mark on their foreheads, thus making of them 'marked men', as Jesus forecast they would be. It could, in fact, have been a mere continuance of a custom established by Judas Maccabeus or, more properly, Judas Hasmon.

The Hasmonean family traced its descent from Judas'

great grandfather Hasmon, or Asmon ... or even Atsmon. Arising in central Galilee, the family consisted of only the tough old High Priest Mattathias and his five equally tough sons, John, Simon, Judas, Eleazar and Jonathan, when it first came to notice, although there might well have been others, and certainly, womenfolk.

Strictly orthodox, as behove their station, the Hasmoneans were head of the course, tribe or clan of Joarib, which was the very first or premier of the twenty-four courses of priestly families which constituted the hierarchy of Judaism and, as such, was the most important and powerful family in Israel. With religion and politics absolutely inseparable in this land where everything was ordained by God, there is little doubt that Mattathias the High Priest was virtually King of Israel though, of course, in those days there was no longer any such office or title. The Hasmoneans were soon to rectify this.

About a decade before the meat cleaver was to flash in the sun, the country had been invaded by the pagan Assyrians under the hated Antiochus Epiphanes, called 'The Image of God'. Naturally enough, this title could scarcely have endeared him to the Jews who refused to permit any art form which represented any living thing or allowed the sacred name of God to be spoken aloud, or even written in full. Instead, they wrote his name as 'YHWH' and figured that anyone who could pronounce that, was entitled to get away with it.

Many centuries later, the Christians both could and did. By the simple expedient of separating the unpronounceable consonants of 'YHWH' with the vowels in the word *'adonai'* (Lord), they created the word 'Yahowah' later smoothed to Jehovah.

As might have been expected there was trouble with the Assyrian invaders from the very start when Antiochus actually destroyed part of the ancient city of Jerusalem to erect a new Greek city in its place. But when he desecrated the Holy Temple of God, it was the end. Horrified, the High Priest and his people withdrew to nearby Modein, where he built and sanctified a new altar to God.

Soon, however, the Jewish religion was totally banned, and the practice of circumcision, which was a Holy Covenant between the Jew and his God, forbidden. In addition, those Jews who refused to worship and to sacrifice to the pagan gods of the Assyrians, were to be killed.

So come and get us, was Mattathias' answer.

Antiochus took him at his word but, unfortunately, the law enforcement officers arrived just as the High Priest and his people were in the midst of their devotions. When the officers started getting tough, the enraged Mattathias snatched up from the altar the sacrificial meat cleaver and split the Assyrian clean through the skull. No doubt, his sons and the rest of the people dealt similarly with the balance of the Assyrians.

Well aware that his life would speedily be forfeit unless he escaped to the safety of the Wilderness of Judea, Mattathias waved the ghastly crimson cleaver above his head and shouted: 'Let everyone who is zealous of the Law and supports God's Covenant, come out with me!'

In that instant were born the Zealots who, later, would support Jesus of the Christian gospels. More than six thousand of his people—the zealous and the faithful—men, women and children with their flocks and their chattels followed Mattathias out into the Wilderness ... and there Antiochus pursued them.

Knowing that the devout Jews held the Sabbath so sacred that not only would they not fight on that Holy day, but wouldn't even defend themselves if attacked, the wily Antiochus, of course, chose that very day to fall upon the Hasmoneans. Faithful to the Law, they refused to lift a finger in defence of their lives, with the result that more than a thousand of them were slaughtered like cattle. The rest escaped across a river.

Judas Maccabeus could count. Five more Sabbaths like this, he must have argued, and we'll all be dead. Is this what God wants of us? Or does he want us to drive out the invaders first? There was only one answer.

Deciding that God was entitled to a full seven day week from the faithful, they grimly awaited the next Sabbath. It came, and so did the Assyrians anticipating another good day's sport, only to discover that the easy slaughter they'd expected ... was their own. Swinging the Holy swords of Righteousness, the Hasmoneans went from victory to victory, gathering support as they went. In less than two years they had rallied the whole nation behind them and Judas—made leader of the Zealots on the death of his father—had captured Jerusalem and cleansed the Temple of all pollution.

In the many battles which followed, both Judas and his

brother Eleazar were slain but the others carried on in turn until the invaders had been chased over Israel's borders which—as was to happen with other enemies in 1967—were re-pegged at the point where the Assyrians stopped running. It was at this time that the nation got its first seaport, Joppa, which has since been all but swallowed by Tel-Aviv.

At the same time, however, the Hasmoneans picked out their own graves for they made a Treaty of Eternal Friendship with an awesome military power called Rome. It took rather less than a hundred years for the Jews to realise that who makes a friend of Rome goes to meet death halfway.

When the Hasmonean's reward came from a grateful nation, it proved to be astonishing. Not only was Simon, their then leader, appointed High Priest but the shape of things to come was clearly heralded by creating him 'Governor' and making both offices hereditary to his sons and his son's sons 'forever or until a trustworthy prophet shall arise'.

This is very probably a reference to the belief that the ancient prophet Elijah would one day be reincarnated not only to herald the coming of the longed for Messiah, but to point him out. It is worth noting that this is precisely what John the Baptist is supposed to have done and men even thought that he was Elijah.

This, perhaps, is as good a time as any to get squared away, once and for all, this dream-figure of the Messiah, which was born out of the despair of three deportations and centuries of pagan invasion and domination.

Seldom has one faith more directly spat in the eye of another's belief than did Christianity when it trumped Judaism's expectation that the Messiah was coming, by proclaiming that he'd already been and gone! Not only did this ridicule the Jewish faith but it took the Messianic office in a vice of such distortion that few Christians today have the slightest idea what the thing meant in the days of Jesus.

'Messiah' is not the name of a person but of an office, in much the same way that 'King' is; in fact, the two mean precisely the same thing and were not only inseparable but interchangeable. As written above, it is merely the English form of the Hebrew 'masiach'—'to anoint'—for, to the Jews, the Messiah would be 'the anointed of God' or, in other words, the King of Israel. The title had nothing of the slightest connection with the supernatural nor did it involve angels or Heavenly spacemen or other grotesque inventions. It had everything to do with a natural born, living Jewish King who would sit on a solid throne set smack on the good earth of the nation; a king who, by bursting the invader's shackles on the Jewish people and booting them into the sea or whatever, would re-establish Righteousness and the Rule of Law and, by so doing, would set up the Kingdom of God on Earth, which meant in Israel.

It cannot be too much emphasised that the Kingdom of God was to be on Earth, not in Heaven. It was by hacking in halves the messianic office and taking only the title—and by discarding all reference to its earthly and only connotation—that Christian theology distorted 'Messiah' into the name of the occupant of a ghost throne in the Kingdom of Heaven. Misused as it is today in the Christian coupling 'Jesus Christ', it is no wonder that the more ignorant Christian imagines this to be Jesus' full name, as his own might be Joe Bloggs. Actually 'Christ' is merely the English form of the Latin 'Christus' which was that language's version of the Greek 'Christos' which, in turn, translated the Hebrew 'masiach'. It's as simple—or as complicated—as that.

Though the original Jewish Messianic expectation involved a King of the Royal House of David, that dream had vanished in the dust of deportation almost five hundred years before. Who knew who was of the royal line? Had David had only a couple of sons and they had had a couple of sons each and so on, the number of lineal male descendants of King David would have far exceeded the present world population and would have made Israel a rather crowded place around 150 B.C. No, the Davidic dream was gone forever and, perhaps, the practical Jews had elected to transfer their Messianic expectation from what was clearly impossible to what was now excitingly possible. However it might have been, it is undeniable that the Hasmoneans were the only foreseeable hope that Israel had that the Messiah would ever arise. It isn't too difficult to see this yearning stirring in the honours heaped on Simon the Hasmonean.

King in all but name, he was to be obeyed by all, and all contracts were to be written in his name. Only he could make official appointments; only he had charge of the nation's defences as well as the Sanctuary; no assembly of the people could be convened without his permission, and only he could wear purple—the royal colour—and only he could wear gold, the royal metal.

The actual decree making these and other pronouncements law was inscribed on tablets of bronze and set up in the Temple Sanctuary, while parchment copies to the same effect were placed in the security of the Treasury 'so that Simon and his sons might have them', presumably, for ever and ever.

It is clear that from this point the Hasmoneans prepared to found a dynasty to wear the Crown of Israel, for when John Hyrcanus, Simon's son, succeeded him he was hailed as Messiah and assumed the title of Prince, and so coins from his era describe him.

It was probably at this time that the Hasmoneans were granted the gift of the nation's most fertile tract of country—the Plain of Gennesareth or, as it might have been called, 'The Garden of the Prince'—and it is to here that we trace home the very first of the claims made by the author of the 'fifteenth scroll'; that he was Jesus of Gennesareth and the last surviving direct lineal descendant of the glorious Hasmonean King's of Israel.

At the same time might also have come the famous balsam gardens near Jericho which, stolen by Herod and from him by Cleopatra—who leased them back to him at a rental of $200,000 a year—must have yielded a fantastic income. With the other gifts might have come 'The King's Garden' although this most probably was a gift made to John Hyrcanus' son, Aristobulus, first openly to assume the title 'King of the Jews' and its variant 'King of Israel'. The tract called 'The King's Garden' was in the Kidron Valley separating the Temple from the Mount of Olives and, through it meandered the brook Kidron, crossed many times by Jesus of the gospels. Within this garden was another—Gethsemane—which seems to have held a peculiar attraction for Jesus, and was the spot chosen when he turned himself in to the Romans. Why here?

Could the reason possibly have been that, for the last time, he wanted to stand on Hasmonean soil?

8 / Herod the Diseased Monster

With the sole exception of Adolf Hitler, no more evil man than Herod can ever have lived; Herod, the King whom history calls 'the Great'. He was great indeed, one of the really great monsters of all time, even in an age noted for them.

His cold-blooded plan was to plunder a throne. To get it, he had to murder the entire Hasmonean Royal Family and their chief male relatives and, having killed to get it he killed to keep it ... slaying his wife, his mother, his sister, uncounted cousins and uncles, three of his own sons, his brother in law, numerous courtiers and servants suspected of plotting against him and literally anyone who even remotely stood between him and his rapacious desires.

Even on his deathbed when, happily, his loins were riddled with cancer and writhing in worms, the monster had the chief men of every city in Israel arrested and herded into Jerusalem's Roman Hippodrome, where guards with drawn swords had the murderous order: 'The moment I die, kill them all. Then all Judea and every family will weep for me; how can they help it?'

Barely a hundred years after the rise of the Hasmoneans the friendly neighbourhood Romans marched into Israel and established the rule of Rome, interrupting a fratricidal battle for the throne between the two Hasmonean brothers, John, who was High Priest, and Aristobulus, who was King. John's adviser and chief backer was a rich and powerful Idumean named Antipater, who had ambitious plans for his handsome son, Herod.

Fed up at last with the bloody bickering between the brotherly rivals for the Hasmonean throne—and having backed each in turn as the occasion demanded—Rome finally abolished the monarchy and stored the vacant throne in a back room ... until needed. John seems to have won the hand, for Rome confirmed him as High Priest but added 'Governor' to his titles. His brother Aristobulus was given ... the headsman's axe in Antioch.

Having successfully lobbied and bribed his way in Rome to be appointed Roman Procurator of Judea—a post which would be held with some distinction some seventy years later by Pontius Pilate—Herod's dad promptly appointed his favourite son Governor of Galilee. While this was stage one of his master plan Galilee could have been no sinecure with the province rolling and boiling as the Hasmonean Zealots built up a full head of royalist steam. Off went Herod to Galilee, his secret plan tucked away in his scheming head.

As Governor, his opening gambit revealed a novel approach; it wasn't to improve the roads or, as any other man might have done, relieve the suffering rich by increasing the taxes on the poor. Deciding to perform a real public duty, he resolved to rid the country of the 'bandits and brigands who infested Galilee'.

Mounting practically a major military campaign he went bald-headed for their leader. Now this man, Hezekiah, might well have been a bad egg; however, he certainly was both a Priest or Rabbi and an important member of the Hasmonean clan.

Pursuing him into the twisted hills above Kana of Galilee—a Zealot settlement and the home of Flavius Josephus the historian—Herod fought a bloody battle with Hezekiah and his Zealots and finally won the day. Many of the band were captured, including their leader. Giving them short shrift and even less mercy or justice, Herod had them beheaded on the spot.

And then, a rather curious thing happened.

Having rid the country of these 'troublesome pests' he was surely entitled to expect a far different reward from the outcry of 'Murder!' which followed the slayings. Whoever heard of a national protest over the killing of a few bandits and brigands?

A clue to whom Hezekiah might have been is provided by what happened next. John Hyrcanus might have been only High Priest and Governor of Israel, and no King, but he came of tough, Hasmonean stock. In short time Herod—powerful son of the most powerful man in the land—found himself in Jerusalem and the dock, on trial for murder. Only the dramatic and probably dearly bought intervention of the Roman Emperor saved golden boy from the axe.

All of which is extremely strange.

In a country and an era when life was held cheap, would John Hyrcanus have risked a showdown with Herod and his powerful father—and an open break with Rome—over the lives of a few paltry criminals? Yet, he did! Both his violent and perilous reaction and the nation-wide outcry strongly suggest that Hezekiah must have been a man of some note, rather than a 'bandit and brigand' and might even have been one of John Hyr-canus' immediate kin.

It took the events of the next hundred years to reveal that Hezekiah had been both a Priest—as were all male Hasmoneans—and a contender for the vacant throne of Israel though whether or not he pressed his claim is un-known. In all probability he did not as the 'weather' was inclined to be inclement. His death, therefore, seems to have been but the necessary first step in Herod's chilling plan to liquidate them all.

Assured of immunity by Caesar's protection, from this time on Herod and his commanders hunted down the vari-ous Zealot groups in which was harboured a Hasmonean 'queen-bee', like rats to be exterminated. They all had royal entitlement and thus must have stood somewhere in the line of succession. Herod and the boys in the back room saw to it that they never made it.

One by one they were picked off and, while his troops winkled out the Hasmonean fringe heirs—'not so much because they claimed the throne', says Josephus, 'but be-cause they were entitled to it!'—Herod was hacking away at the two main contenders. These were the now ageing John Hyrcanus and his nephew Antigonus, son of the man who lost his head in Antioch.

Trounced in a battle with Antigonus' forces—Zealots to a man, you can be certain—Herod fled whimpering to Rome leaving the delirious Jews to proclaim the victor High Priest and King of Israel.

In Rome, meanwhile, Herod was wheedling and bribing his way into Caesar's good graces and made such a good job of it that he got what he had coveted for years, the Throne of Israel. To occupy it, all he had to do was wrench it away from its rightful owner, Antigonus. Three years and several bloody battles later, he made it.

Antigonus was sent in chains to suffer in Rome the fate his father had met in Antioch, and Herod was the master of Judea. Then this astonishing schemer whose hide was evidently thick enough to turn a spear at ten paces, turned his wife out of the palace and married the beautiful Miriamne (Mary) who was none other than the grand daughter of old John Hyrcanus. As she is reported to have hated him as passionately as he loved her, Herod's use of threats and all kinds of duress can be presumed. Now not only was he King, but related to the Hasmoneans by marriage; the birth of an heir would surely placate the Jewish nation's hate. It did not. The Jews wanted none of this bastard half-Jew or his progeny; they wanted their true Messiah, who could come only from the mainline Hasmoneans.

Few, however, were left . . . except for Miriamne's 16 year old brother.

Herod had him appointed High Priest and, a few days later, ordered him drowned in the swimming pool. A couple of years later, when the banished and doddering John Hyrcanus was foolish enough to visit Jerusalem for the Passover, Herod had him strangled. With the short list of Hasmonean heirs entirely cancelled, all that remained were a few no-hopers whom Herod thought would never give him any trouble, the King was free to turn his murderous attention to his own family, with the results already related.

That the remaining—or surviving—Hasmoneans constituted no threat to the now ageing Herod is thrown into doubt by two highly important events which occurred a year or two before the diseased horror's welcome death in 4 B.C.

John the Baptist and Jesus were born . . . and a Hasmonean Zealot, called Judas the Galilean, assembled a force and attacked the state capital of Sepphoris. By what seems to have been a curious coincidence, this Judas was the son of that murdered Hezekiah whose death years before, had very nearly cost Herod his head. The dying King smelled the danger even in his malodorous sickroom, and his vengeance was both swift and merciless.

His troops stormed into Sepphoris and captured the 'upstart', then, accusing the city of collusion with the rebels, General Varus destroyed and burned it, laying it utterly waste. Judas and no less than 2000 of his men were crucified on a forest of crosses. Historically, this was the very first time that crucifixion was made the official punishment for bandits and brigands, *and specifically was it reserved for Zealot rebels and those whose royalist aspirations they supported.*

Christians might care to ponder on this!

However, despite the frightful penalty for failure the Hasmoneans never ceased their periodic and fanatical efforts to regain their Throne. Fifty years after Judas died on the cross at Sepphoris, his sons James and Simon suffered exactly the same fate for exactly the same reason.

The collapse of Herod's dynasty of Kings into the mere state governors that his heirs became, and Rome's appointment of Procurators to govern Judea as a whole, provided the climate for restoration and many more attempts must have been made than those recorded by Josephus.

It seems quite evident that as each Hasmonean survivor rose to the top of the heap, he either had to make a bid for the throne or relinquish his rights. Not even the almost certain failure that awaited his bid in the very shadow of the cross evidently deterred the 'next Hasmonean', for fulfilment of the Jewish Messianic expectation was seen as a command from God.

On the human level, the prize was a compelling—even a tempting—attraction. Untold riches, King of all Israel ... and, perhaps, beyond; honour, adulation, power and the confidences of other Kings are all tasty tidbits on the banquet table of life and few can resist their blandishments. Few did!

With the sole exception of the ill-fated Mennahem whose shot at the Throne was marked by the Jewish War that flared in its train, and Simon ben Kosebah's rebellion in 132 A.D., we don't definitely know of any further restoration attempts. Reason suggests that there must have been others which, perhaps because they were nipped in the bud, failed to make the only history book that has come down to us. Little is known about what seems to have been the Hasmonean's last despairing effort, the Kosebah rebellion.

What is known for certain is that he was a Hasmonean and that he styled himself, and was accepted as, 'Prince of Israel' and Messiah, and was popularly known as 'Son of the Star'. It seems that this was no mere symbolic title but a direct reference to his 'city' or the area where he lived, just as Jesus of Nazareth's, Joseph of Arimathea's, or Jesus of Gennesareth's were to theirs. While a Jew's reference to himself as the son of his father had value at the village or town level, it had little revelance should he journey to other parts of the country. In this case, strangers wanted to know where a man came from, rather than the name of his father. And so it was that, for example, the author of the 'fifteenth scroll' called himself 'Jesus son of Gennesareth son of Jacob'; he put the least important information last. And Simon, 'Son of the Star' did precisely the same, which enables us to say with great confidence that he was a Hasmonean pretender.

'Simon son of the star son of Kosebah' translates into the Hebrew *'Shimeon ben Kaukab ben Kosebah'*, and *Kaukab* (the star) is still the name of a village in Israel today. There it is in Galilee, squatting but two miles west of the Hasmonean stronghold of Jotapata.

Just as Josephus tells us nothing about Kosebah, because he died thirty years before that rebellion, so he tells us nothing about a similar attempt at the Hasmonean restoration that occurred a few years before he was born; an event whose minor nature failed to attract the historian's attention.

Almost certainly we have a sketchy record of this in the gospels and, perhaps, another exists in the scroll of Jesus of Gennesareth.

9 / The Forgotten King

'Repent ye, for the Kingdom of God is at hand!' When the wild looking figure called John the Baptist came stalking out of the Wilderness of Judea, clad in animal skins and eating roast locusts and wild honey, he was already a figure of mystery.

From his raiment, diet and utterances modern scholars seem confident that they correctly place John as an expelled member of the sectarian Essenes whose ruined monastery at Qumran—reputed to be the site of ancient, sinful Gomorrah—once housed the Dead Sea Scrolls.

The sect's 'Manual of Discipline' provided total excommunication for a variety of crimes, one of which earned for the offending brother what was virtually a sentence of death. Thrown out into the arid desert but not released from his solemn vows never to dwell among men or even share their food, the outcast either had to live off the land—eating what nature and providence sent him—or starve to a miserable death. Oddly enough, Josephus claims to have once been a member of the Essene sect and to have studied under a hermit-like figure named Bannus, which means 'baptiser', although there is no suggestion that this man might actually have been John.

How did it happen that this cousin of Jesus became a member of this strange sect?

The answer is fascinating ... and, to a major degree, speculative although it is probably very close to the truth. Although John's origin appears to be clearly stated in the gospels, it is surrounded by exactly the same hocus-pocus which is found in the story of Jesus' conception and birth. Oddly enough, both infants are lost sight of soon after birth until they emerge on to the Judean stage some thirty or so years later. Nor is the enigma helped by the plain truth that we don't for certain know when either was born or died; we can only work between broad limits which, in each case, might be as much as a whole decade away from the true date.

The riddle of John and of who and what he was, begins in the 1st chapter of *Luke:* 'There was in the days of Herod, King of Judea, a certain priest named Zacharias of the course (family) of Abia, and his wife was of the daughters of Aaron and her name was Elizabeth.'

We stop right there, for immediately we're in deep trouble.

The priesthood of Israel was divided into twenty-four courses by King David at about 1000 B.C. Four hundred years later Persia overran the nation and deported all its chief men and their families to Babylon. Released after seventy years and allowed to return to Jerusalem, four of the homecoming priestly families who tried to resume their former authority, ran into difficulties. As the Scripture says: 'These sought their register among those that were reckoned by genealogy, but it was not found. Therefore were they, as polluted, put from the priesthood . . .' The sentence imposed on the four unfortunate families— one of which was Abia—meant that they were excluded for ever and ever.

Yet here we find the priestly father of John the Baptist—a member of the excluded family of Abia—serving in the Temple.

While the error doesn't make the whole passage suspect, it does suggest that an editorial tamperer had been at work and, either through carelessness or ignorance, had altered Zacharias' true course to one designed to conceal it. As Abia was very close kin to the course of Joarib— they both having had a common ancestor—and Joarib was the course of the Hasmoneans, perhaps there was a good motive for the editorial change, which must have been to conceal the fact that Zacharias was a Hasmonean.

Luke continues, and in 1:8-10 says: 'And it came to pass that while he executed the priest's office before God in the order of his course—according to the custom of the priest's office, his lot was to burn incense when he went into the Temples of the Lord—and the whole multitude of the people were praying without at the time of incense.'

Strangely constructed though those verses are, they provide a wealth of astonishing information. To start at the end, 'the time of incense' definitely identifies the occasion as the Day of Atonement, which tells us a great deal.

Although the burning of incense was once the sole prerogative of the High Priest, by this time all priests had been admitted to this service, with the important exception that, on the Day of Atonement, the burning was still restricted to the High Priest. This was the one day of the year when only he was permitted to enter the Holy of Holies—the gospelist's 'Temple of the Lord'—where, protected from the Divine Wrath by the burning incense, he made atonement before God for the past year's sins of the people of Israel. The fact that Zacharias had both burned the incense on this day and had entered the Holy of Holies clearly reveals him as High Priest of Israel. This is confirmed by the gospel author's use of the singular-possessive priest's office' *twice* instead of the plural-possessive 'priests' office', which would have applied to the general priesthood. Undoubtedly, the word 'high' must once have stood before 'priest's' but, as has so often happened, came to the attention of an editor bent on deleting the truth.

The discovery that Zacharias was High Priest means much more than it might seem to; that he was a Hasmonean is certain and, being the husband of Elizabeth who was the Virgin's cousin, the chances are that it had been Zacharias who had had the blood relationship rather than his wife. If correct, this would have made him cousin by blood to either Mary or her husband—probably the latter as these things were noticed only through the male line—and made it likely that both Alpheus and his brother Joseph were also Hasmoneans. However, the intriguing passage has even wider repercussions.

For example, it would explain a mystery concerning James, the brother of Jesus, drawn attention to by Eusebius, who quoted his predecessor, Hegesippus as follows: 'James, the brother of the Lord, was holy from his mother's womb ... to him only was it permitted to enter the Holy of Holies ...' Although the full quotation is not given here, enough has been quoted to elicit the astonishing information that James was actually High Priest of the Temple of Judaism at the same time that he was head of the Nazorean-Christian Church in Jerusalem. It is probably this embarrassing news—so far unexplained by the Church—which has caused most sectarian commentators to omit the phrase: 'to him only was it permitted to enter the Holy of Holies' on the rare occasions when they even refer to the passage.

Hegesippus adds that James was violently killed when he was dashed from the pinnacle of the Temple and stoned to death in the Kidron Valley below. The event is confirmed by Josephus who, in a more detailed account, relates that the High Priest Ananus brought charges against James and certain others before the Sanhedrin which, finding them guilty, delivered them over to be stoned to death. Although the charges are not defined, it was for the crime of causing the death of James that King Agrippa removed Ananus from office; it is not impossible, therefore, that the dispute might actually have been over which of the two was entitled to the High Priesthood and so, no more than just another power struggle.

Given that Hegesippus' story is true, how could James possibly have come to the High Priesthood?

The most likely way is by inheritance.

If old Zacharias—whom we have left still wreathed in the sweet smoke of incense—had been High Priest, his right to the office would have been inherited by his son, John the Baptist. With John dead, the title could have passed to Jesus' father—and from him, given some disqualifying blemish—to Jesus. If so, then after the Crucifixion, the office and title might have passed to James by default of any living son of Jesus.

Led by the scent of incense, we rejoin Zacharias in the Temple. Here, we are told, he was startled to see an angel of the Lord who announced that—old as Zacharias was, and barren though his wife had proved—they were soon to be blessed by God with a son. It is no wonder that the old Priest was immediately struck dumb and never spoke again until the promised son's circumcision on the traditional eighth day. As he vanishes from the story at this point, it is presumed that his dumbness might have been due to a stroke—which finally carried him off—brought on by his overenthusiastic efforts both to anticipate the angel's promise and to render it superfluous.

However, this supposition might be very far from the truth in view of the strong early tradition that Zacharias had been slain between the Temple and the Brazen Altar ... by King Herod the Great!

True or not—and more than half-a-dozen of the early Fathers of the Church accepted it without dispute—the tradition resulted in Zacharias being made a Martyr of the Christian Church, and what was reputed to have been his head was actually exhibited and venerated in the Lateran Basilica in Rome.

Fact or fiction, our knowledge of Herod suggests that he probably had the best reason in the world to kill the High Priest; producing an heir at that late stage in his life. Aware that Zacharias was a Hasmonean, he might have been content to let him live merely because the old man constituted no danger, having no heir. And now, the old fake had tricked him. One can almost see the enraged Herod, wracked with pain from his disease and purple with anger, meeting—or even seeking out—Zacharias in the Temple precincts and slaying the frail figure with one blow of his sword.

We are persuaded to accept the story because of what followed next, but before passing to it reference must be made to another curious tradition which maintains that much of what the gospels have to say about the infant Jesus historically concerned his cousin, the infant John, six months his elder. In fact, it is said that there is still to be found—or, was until recent times—an ancient sect called Mandeans who inhabited the area of the Lower Euphrates, who bitterly denounce Jesus as a fake and claim that John, not Jesus, had been the true Messiah and King; what is more, they claim to possess ancient documents to prove it.

With all these bits and pieces of a broken jigsaw to assemble, we come now to what has become known as 'The Slaughter of the Innocents'—the 'Deadly Ernest' horror of one's earliest Sunday school days.

Although dismissed by most scholars as a fiction— mainly only because Josephus fails to mention it—the killing of the children of Bethlehem might eventually come to be seen as one of the most historically true incidents in the entire gospels.

Related only by *Matthew*, the story has it that at some unknown time after the birth of Jesus certain Wise Men came prowling around the bazaars of Jerusalem asking: 'Where is he that is born King of the Jews?' If it happened historically, then what the men were really asking was where they'd find the child recently born into the family first in line for the usurped throne of the Hasmoneans. No other interpretation is possible nor will 'King of the Jews' permit of any tampering. It meant what it said and carried absolutely no connotation of a spiritual king or leader.

The men's enquiries were overheard by Herod's vast spy ring and reported back, possibly with the babe's father identified. Naturally enough, the news threw the diseased king into a frenzy, so that he grabbed his sword and headed for the Temple and old Zacharias. The rest, possibly we know.

The tradition that Herod killed Zacharias dies hard and there must have been some reason for its arising. If it happened, Herod must have had some motive for killing him and the birth of this heir might have been it.

As the gospel story stands now—applied to the infant Jesus—the connotation was that this was a spiritual king that had been born. Rest assured, had Herod understood that he would merely have resumed his scratching at his worms and ordered the killing of another relative. It was earthly, sword swinging kings that Herod had his nightmares about, a restoration of the Hasmoneans; about that and only that!

Too late, perhaps, Herod regretted his impetuosity for, although he knew the father, Herod had made the mistake of striking before he had elicited the vital information concerning the child's whereabouts. Old Zacharias must have been fully aware of the danger and have sent Elizabeth and the infant to a place safely out of the monster-King's reach. He died with his secret.

The wily and superstitious Herod decided to match guile with guile; he consulted the Sanhedrin and asked where, in the Sacred Scriptures, the prophets said the Messiah was to be born? Innocently quoting *Micah* 5:2, they smiled and said: 'Bethlehem!'

The result was a horror to chill the blood!

Sending in the troops, a house-to-house search was made for the child—which one is uncertain—and finding plenty of infants but none which parents or neighbours thought was the Messiah, decided to kill them all and thus make certain that his quarry would not escape. And so, according to *Matthew*, it was done!

But was it? Despite its similarity to the tale told of the jealous rajahs seeking to kill the infant Krishna, there would seem to be no good reason why the same thing might not have happened, given the same circumstances. Royal infanticide was not all that unusual. Furthermore, it has the unmistakable reek of Herod the monstrous and, though one realises the subjectivity of the decision, I would be inclined to believe the incident historical. But was it John or Jesus that the King was after?

As we don't know precisely when the two were born or when the massacre is supposed to have taken place, it is entirely possible that—being six months the younger—Jesus wasn't even born at the time. Although the story seems to require that the child must have been two years old, this might merely have been a case of Herod giving himself plenty of margin for error. Additionally, the abrupt disappearance of Zacharias immediately after John's circumcision and the tradition that he was killed by Herod, combine to suggest that the slaughter occurred soon after those events.

Furthermore, the strangers' enquiry: 'Where is he that is born King of the Jews?' implies either that the child was King when born or, more reasonably, that he was King at the time the enquiry was made; the latter fits a ten-days-old John who might recently have been made fatherless. A child who was King at the time the enquiry was made rules out Jesus for, quite apart from the strong possibility that he hadn't then been born, Jesus could have inherited only by the death of John some thirty or so years later.

So, seeing John as the quarry rather than Jesus, where might he have been when the Bethlehem massacre took place?

Tradition nominated Beth Haccerem—the modern Ein Kerem—about three miles from Jerusalem as John's birthplace, although with what authority is unknown. In any case, the place of his birth is not as important as his whereabouts a couple of weeks after. The gospel of *Luke* might provide a clue when it says, in 1:80: '*And the child* grew and waxed strong in spirit and *was in the desert* until the day of his showing unto Israel.'

Obviously this doesn't mean that he spent the next thirty years under a palm tree, and can only mean that Elizabeth must have reached the place of refuge to which shrewd old Zacharias had sent her with the babe shortly before his death . . . which he must have anticipated.

What place?

As it was from the Wilderness of Judea that John had emerged 'on the day of his showing unto Israel', it can only be assumed that it had been into the same desert wasteland that he had vanished with his mother thirty years before. Logic suggests that the place of refuge was Qumran, the settlement of the royalist-partisan Essenes.

There, getting on in years and no doubt greatly weakened by a difficult labour late in life and grieving for her dead husband, the courageous Elizabeth had probably slid into death leaving the infant John and his secret to the care of the solicitous monks.

Josephus tells us that one of the Essenes' most notable customs was the adoption of other men's children for, eschewing marriage, they constantly replenished their numbers by this device. However, lest it be thought that they were a group of frustrated sex-starved celibates—as most Christian clerics have been for almost two thousand years, unless they're cheating—marriage was permitted to a select few, but strictly for childbearing only. It might well have been that among their wives the orphaned John's foster-mother was found and, among their children, his playmates.

And so, according to our hypothesis built out of the evidence of the gospels, such history as exists and traditions of great age and tenacity—which is all that the gospel stories themselves really are—he who was born King of the Jews and Messiah of Israel eluded the dripping swords of Herod and dwelt in safety and anonymity for some thirty years ... until the day came when he offended against his vows and was expelled from the Essene community to fend for himself in the desert.

How long John wandered in the desert is, of course, unknown but at last, probably deranged by privation but certainly inspired, the wild figure staggered out of that wilderness of scorpions, his crazed and cracked voice shouting to the ears of a sinful Israel: 'Prepare ye the way of the Lord; make his paths straight!"

And one of the first to hear the words was his long-lost cousin ... Jesus!

10 / Rivals for the Throne of Israel

'John did baptise in the Wilderness . . . and it came to pass that Jesus came . . . and was baptised of John in Jordan.'

In such deceptively innocent phrases do the gospels dismiss a great human drama that must have surrounded the meeting of these two central figures who were both cousins and strangers. So far as we are told, they had never before set eyes on each other yet, instantly John recognised Jesus—if not as cousin—as one in authority over him for he said: 'I have need to be baptised of *thee!'*

One can please oneself, of course, whether or not one accepts that speech as authentic and a reflection of the true nature of events. However, from its implication that John had, by some mysterious means, instantly recognised Jesus as Divine leads to the suspicion that an editorial hand had been at work, for it amounts to little more than an injection into the past of doctrine that only arose subsequent to the Resurrection.

Given the historicity of that speech, and ruling out all supernatural prescience on John's part, what did it mean and how did he arrive at his opinion of Jesus' superiority? Before attempting answers, we shall have to find one to an even more intriguing question: what was it that brought John out of the desert? In short, what was his object?

The gospels see him as the herald of the future Messiah—analogous to the character who races onstage saying: 'Here come de Judge!'—and do their best to suggest that the people saw John as the reincarnation of the prophet Elijah, as indeed they probably did. However that might have been, it still does not provide an answer to what might have motivated the recluse.

Was he splashed by the bubbling cauldron of Messianic expectation that was on the boil, stoked as it was by all Israel's hate of the Romans? Or had he a deeper and more personal motive?

Civilisation has a very ancient and very wise proverb which particularly applies to the gospels: 'Actions speak louder than words!' It is suggested that it is by what John *did,* rather than by what he is alleged to have said by subsequent authors and editors intent on aggrandising Jesus as the future God, that we might best measure John's 'mission'.

It is apparent that he came out of the desert and immediately embarked on the recruitment of supporters by 'baptising' them in the Jordan. For what? So that they would be acceptable to the coming God? Or so that they would be 'acceptable' to the coming one who, as we shall see, was almost ready to make his bid to regain the throne for the Hasmoneans and become King and Messiah?

Baptism wasn't a Johanine innovation, as many are led to believe; not only did the Essenes require it but the Priests of the Temple in Jerusalem were obliged to plunge beneath the waters daily, the Essenes before every meal. These were all probably meant to be ceremoniously purifying rather than of any deep spiritual significance and, if so, were entirely different from the baptism of new adherents to Judaism. Both, it seems, were quite different from John's sacrament of baptism, whose precise nature still baffles objective scholars. Everyone knows the meaning invested in it by the gospels, but what was its meaning to John?

In the early 1st century the general meaning of 'sacrament' was none other than 'a soldier's oath of loyalty and allegiance', and was usually made by the individual before the person of the King or leader to whom it was being sworn. So that the suspicion exists that John might have been forming the nucleus of an army—even an army itself—to support the claims of the man destined to snatch back the throne and become the Messiah. Just who it was who John saw in this role will be discussed later.

It is quite certain that he had surrounded himself with disciples very early in the story—two of whom were Simon called Peter and his brother, Andrew—though whether or not these 'disciples' should be seen as a group of paramilitary advisers and experts in guerilla war or merely a bodyguard, is open to argument.

What is also quite certain is that John was, in fact, baptising soldiers as *Luke* 3:14 testifies. So that we are entitled, on the evidence, to see John's baptism as the recruitment of supporters or troops whose defilement caused by their earlier allegiance was washed away by the waters of Jordan, whereupon the baptised then swore a new oath of allegiance.

To whom?

Assume that the long-hidden John was perfectly well aware of who and what he was; that his mother Elizabeth had entrusted the Essenes with his secret, which was later told to John. Aware of his destiny which, one can be sure, was pointed out to him by the royalist sectarians, John might have seen his expulsion as a sign from God that this was his moment of truth. So that when he came stalking out of the Wilderness proclaiming: 'Prepare the way of the Lord; make his paths straight!' he might have seen himself as no mere herald, but as the future Messiah!

Clearly, the authorities were suspicious of his motives for 'the Jews sent Priests and Levites (guards or soldiers) from Jerusalem to ask him: "Who art thou?" And he confessed, and denied not; but confessed, "I am not the Messiah!"' Well, nobody but a fool would have admitted such a role, with its connotation of violence and conflict with the Romans and their Jewish sycophants. Away went the Priests and their troops, apparently satisfied that they had nothing to fear, at least, from this man.

Then cometh Jesus. Why?

Did he come out of idle curiosity, or was it something more? Evidently it was the latter for the gospel stresses that he had come to be baptised, which means that he had decided to support John. In what? If John was recruiting, then Jesus' coming to join the movement is *prima facie* evidence that John was staking his claim. While this might have been so, it could hardly have been a desire to *join* John which had brought him to the banks of the Jordan.

The fact that Jesus was arrested, tried and executed for claiming to have been 'King of the Jews' (Israel) suggests that he must long have held both the right to sue for the Throne and the expectation that there was no other—or better—contender. He might even have been brought up to regard himself as Israel's future King-elect, for with the presumed death in infancy of John, the inheritance evidently passed to the family of Jesus.

So that when he heard that there was a former hermit posing as the Messiah and recruiting forces at the Jordan, Jesus might have felt compelled to investigate.

There seems to be no doubt that Jesus' 'royalty' was an open secret of the times. The days had long passed when even *being* a Hasmonean meant death; the survivors of the family were suffered to exist but a wary eye was kept on them and they had to make only one false step in the direction of their former Throne for the authorities to act. So that when Jesus came to the Jordan men whispered his identity in John's ear. Immediately, dull-witted John was perplexed. How could he be the Messiah if Jesus were? Then arose the most amusing situation reported in *Matthew* 3:13-15 in which the two argue as to who should join whom. John's uncertainty about their relative positions in the Hasmonean hierarchy is plainly evident, and he was only partly reassured when Jesus elected to join John's forces and 'suffered himself for now' to be baptised. This, of course, can mean nothing less than that Jesus saw it as a temporary arrangement; possibly he considered John's movement a convenient screen to his own aspirations.

No clear picture is possible of what really happened at Jesus' baptism, for the incident is obscured by fantasy and theological symbolism. We are told that God's voice is heard giving his 'son' a verbal pat on the head and as a sign of the presence of the Divine Spirit, a dove 'descends' on Jesus. Fantastic? Perhaps there is a grain of truth in it, mangled though it might be. However, what is particularly significant in the proceedings is that the words said to have been spoken by God derive, in fact, from the 2nd Psalm ... which was the identical one used in the coronation ceremonies of the Hasmonean Kings and Messiahs!

Interesting though this is, it is in the dove symbol that the most intriguing field for investigation lies. The dove had long been of great religious significance in Judaism. Millions were sacrificed annually in the Temple at Jerusalem and, curiously, most of them were specifically bred for this purpose at the little Galilean village of Midgal, Magadan or Magdala which stood on the Plain of Gennesareth. The revenue which this earned for the reputed home of Mary Magdalene was so vast that a cart had to be used to transport the 'city's' taxes each year to Jerusalem.

Attention has already been drawn to the almost certain possibility that Jesus and his followers bore, somewhere on their bodies, the ancient 'magic' sign which had been long-used by the Hebrews to ward-off physical—and, perhaps, spiritual—harm. Believed to have been the especial sign or charm of the Maccabeans or Hasmoneans, it consisted of the Hebrew letter 'tau', 'taw' or 'tav', which was shaped like the Cross of later Christianity. While it suggested that the Hasmoneans had worn this cross on their foreheads, their consequent persecution might have driven it off that conspicuous place, to one 'underground' and, perhaps, on their chests.

Is it possible that, by this time, the persecuted Hasmonean heirs had not only changed the position of their magic charm, but had also changed its form? Could the form used at the time of Jesus have been a dove with outstretched wings? This would still have retained sufficient resemblance to a Hebrew 'taw' still to contain the same significance for its wearers, yet would be sufficiently different to escape comment. The fact that Judaism forbade the use of tattooing would not have prevented the Hasmoneans from resorting to it; after all, the Law had not prevented them from fighting on the Sabbath.

The suspicion that we might well be on the right track is reinforced by the fact that one of the Hebrew nouns for dove is 'tor', which is phonetically identical with 'taw', meaning a cross.

All four gospels agree that the Holy Spirit descended upon Jesus *like* a dove, and nowhere state that a living dove actually flew at him or perched on his head.

In the gospel of *John*, Jesus three times in a few seconds addresses Simon Peter—one of John the Baptist's original disciples—as 'bar yonah', which has usually been read as 'son of Jonah' or 'son of John'. Now, it seems, the experts might have been wrong.

Would you believe that the second Hebrew noun for dove was 'yonah'? Jesus called Simon Peter's attention to the fact that he was a 'Son of the Dove'—and three times reminding him of it—might have been to emphasise that, as a member of a clandestine group, the sign he bore imposed certain obligations which he was expected to carry out.

In fact, it could have been the 'Sign of the Dove' on each other's chests when Jesus and John stripped for the immersion of baptism, that had caused each to recognise the other. If so, while impetuous John immediately accepted a lower rung on the ladder and had confessed it, Jesus had remained silent, and had suffered himself to be sworn in as John's liege man.

Almost immediately after his baptism, we are told, Jesus did something which has never been satisfactorily explained and which stands in the gospels wreathed in symbolical fantasy and nonsense.

'Then was Jesus led up of the Spirit into the Wilderness to be tempted of the devil.'

What does this passage really mean? Is it sheer symbolism or does it describe a real event? Or is it a mixture of both? Divorced from all superstition it can only mean that Jesus withdrew to consider his position: should he throw in his lot with John and support him in his attempt at the Hasmonean restoration, or should he go it alone?

Consider the situation as it probably stood. After some thirty years of regarding himself as Israel's future King-Messiah, he had suddenly discovered the long lost true heir, John ben Zacharias. What should he do? Tell the unbalanced John that it was all a mistake? that he, Jesus, was the true heir to the Hasmoneans? With such a simpleton, one could tell him anything. Could Israel's future be entrusted to such a one? Any attempt at the restoration by John was not only foredoomed to failure but might result in a frightful persecution which, this time, might eliminate the Hasmonean line for ever. What was best for Israel? What did God want Jesus to do? Obviously, one of them had to go, but which? But was there any choice, unless it was obvious? From this mountain top Jesus could look far into the distance; under his leadership there was no limit to the extent to which Israel's borders might be stretched. Could John do all that?

If this, in fact, was what the incident was all about, historically—and it's difficult to see what else it *could* have been about—what was Jesus' solution to the problem?

Remember that we are speaking here about a real, historical man and *not* the idealised God of perfection into which Christian theology swiftly turned him. Jesus was fully human and subject to exactly the same temptations as other men. To suggest that he might have been frail enough not to be able to resist temptation, is a speculation about the man of history and no criticism of the God of theology.

Who is to say that, historically, Jesus did not succumb to temptation?

The various gospel accounts of what followed the temptation differ; however, it is quite evident that there must have been a blazing quarrel between the rivals and that they split and each went his way. Perhaps significantly, two of John's disciples quit to join Jesus and make it plain that they regarded him as the true Messiah.

As far as it can be calculated, it was immediately after the quarrel that John the Baptist was arrested and imprisoned in the fortress of Machaerus, east of the Jordan. According to the story, he was arrested for spreading the slander that Herod Antipas was committing incest with his brother Philip's wife, who had moved in to Machaerus with her daughter, Salome.

That Antipas was doing so is beyond all doubt, but that he would have given a Smyrna fig for the ravings of a half-crazed man of the desert is entirely unlikely. The Herodians were used to far more complicated domestic geometrical figures to worry about a simple triangle or the gossip it aroused. After all, his father, Herod the Great, had not only had a dozen wives, innumerable concubines and the passing maiden, but had gone for the boys, too. No, that slander-tale just doesn't sit well with history.

What would have sent a rush of purple into Herod Antipas' face, however, would have been the news that the harmless crazyman of the desert was not only not as crazy as was thought but, in fact, was actually heir to the Hasmonean Throne. This news would have resulted in John's speedy arrest and death, which is exactly what happened.

The tale of Herodias' daughter, Salome, performing a lascivious dance in return for the gift of John the Baptist's head can be discarded into the same bin as Jack and the Beanstalk. At the time, Salome was a respectably married woman and, as such, would not have been permitted to dance in 'public', even had she dared.

So arises the question: was the 'news' of John's identity and of his plan to stage his bid for the Throne of the Hasmoneans 'leaked' to Antipas?

There is little doubt that Jesus was under great temptation and, offensive though it will be to many, the circumstantial evidence suggests that he yielded to its pressure.

The curious thing is that the very moment John was arrested, Jesus fled. Why? What had he said about Antipas to make him fear for his life? Nothing, as far as we know. However, in view of the probable historical reason for the

Baptist's arrest, then—and only then—Jesus' flight makes very real sense. From the moment of John's death by beheading, Jesus was very certainly the next in line. Was it for fear of his life that Jesus fled north? Or did he flee from his conscience?

The only real hindrance to acceptance of the foregoing hypothesis is—for Christians—the sheer inability to imagine that Jesus could possibly have done such a thing. This, it is respectfully suggested, amounts to little more than a pulling of the sheets of faith over the head of reason so that the horrible fact that the historical Jesus was a fully human man of his times would 'go away'.

As a test of the utter lack of objectivity of such an attitude imagine that, instead of Jesus, some ordinary man of those times had been involved in the same events with the same result. Would it be believed that *he* could have done such things? Alas, we all realise only too well something of the real nature of man. It is worth remembering, sometimes, that Jesus was a man before he became a God.

As a final curious fact in the drama of the episode involving John the Baptist, the change in Jesus after the death of his cousin is remarkable. The aimless drifting about the country on a never-described and seemingly purposeless 'mission' is gone. There is now purpose and resolution and a suddenly found weight of confidence and authority in all his utterances. It would be absurd not to imagine that this, in some way, was connected with John's death.

It might even have been due to the fact that John, in all truth, had indeed 'made straight the way of the Lord' and that nothing—or anyone—now stood between Jesus and his inheritance for he was now, in fact as well as in name, the 'King of the Jews'. All that he lacked to make the great Hasmonean dream come true, was the Throne and that fault he promptly proceeded to attempt to correct.

Such are the quirks of fate that, had he succeeded he would, today, be remembered—if at all—as merely another minor Jewish king. And now men call him God.

11 / Was Jesus Married?

Origen, the famous 3rd century theologian, read too literally a remark by St. Paul and, in a flush of enthusiasm for a permanently celibate life, took a knife and castrated himself. Far too late he knew he had solved nothing for, while the urge was still there, he had done away with his means of satisfying it.

The theologian's extraordinary action was but an extreme example of the remarkable revulsion against sex—particularly heterosex—that was sweeping through the Church in the train of Virgin worship. So desirous was it to set Mary far above all other women, that these they denigrated and reviled in the most degrading and often disgusting terms, placing first male celibacy and finally male virginity as not only desirable, but necessary states if one were to live in Christ.

It is altogether frightening to read the concepts of many of the early great men of the Church, and to realise that these only too clearly revealed their originator's mental and sexual hangups and how often, instead of with Christian love, their minds had seethed with hatred. Often, it was the concepts of such men—although most others were of opposite character—which formed the basis of some subsequent doctrine, boasting much faith and little reason, which still imposes the heavy burden of its incredibility on the faithful of the 20th century.

It is to two of these women-haters—if they were nothing more—the 2nd century heretics Tatian and Basilides, that we owe the utterly historically unfounded and socially and religiously unlikely belief that Jesus had never married, expressed as the dogma of his Perpetual Virginity. At the same time as this absurdity was sprouting in the Church, their contemporary Marcion was hacking away at sex. He limited the sacraments of baptism and the eucharist to virgins, widows and married couples 'who agree together to repudiate marital consummation'. But the frustrated Marcion—who personally never indulged—went to what would seem to be the outer limits of faith by prohibiting marriage for all Christians. In his day, you had your choice, married or Christian. One couldn't be both!

In later centuries, bowing both to the wind and the inevitable, the Church relaxed Marcion's policy—which might have depopulated the world—and settled for marriage for the weak in the flock and celibacy for the strong and therefore Holy others. This, of course, was later expanded into the *demand* that the congregation marry, while for the clergy, nothing changed. Certain of them must have rubbed their hands with glee!

What the Doctrine of Jesus' Perpetual Virginity did was more than muck up this aspect of his historical life, it took him completely out of the world of Judaism and destroyed his visa because, to this extent, it denied that he had ever existed as a human. Which is nonsense, nonsense, nonsense!

To a very large extent, marriage is what Judaism is all about. The sacrifice of the male foreskin—and Jesus did this, too—was more than a covenant with God; its sexual overtones became a sacred promise that the male penis would be put to God's service in the generation of children. Now whether the Church likes it or not, that was what Jesus' circumcision on the 8th day was all about. Though unable to speak, he offered up his foreskin in a Holy promise to God and, if we are able to believe the Church, he broke that promise!

In Jesus' days, every Jewish father was bound by the *Torah* and the duties it imposed; his obligation to his son was five-fold: 'He must circumcise him, redeem him, teach him *Torah*, teach him a trade, and find a wife for him.' Not only was marriage both legally and socially demanded, but avoidance was considered a curse and childlessness a mark of God's distinct disfavour.

With a boy a man at thirteen years old, he was expected to marry at some age between sixteen and twenty. If, however, he still failed to marry, the Holy One said: 'Let him rot!' This was no light curse, either, because an unmarried man was such a rarity that he was usually so odd as to be avoided and probably became an outcast.

Being both a creature of his times and a man of the people, it is fantastic to have evolved a doctrine denying

Jesus' sexuality when the laws and customs of the land saw to it that a youth's sexuality was put to proper use at the very first opportunity and, moreover, there is abundant evidence that Jesus was no exception.

Although the first thirty—or even forty—years of his life appear to be blank, they are not so completely so that we haven't an important record of one of its major events. While all the 'laundry-marks' have been editorially removed to conceal the identity of the chief participants in the function, the circumstances of the wedding at Kana are such that it can be confidently asserted that the bridegroom was none other but Jesus, himself.

That he was, indeed, married is made quite certain by the revelation (*Luke* 8:1-3) that he wandered about the country with an entourage which included 'many women who *ministered unto him of their substance*'.

Bluntly put, the phrase actually means that Jesus and his disciples were being financially supported—and *kept*—by this group of women among whom were a mysterious Susanna, a runaway wife named Joanna, and Mary called Magdalene, whom a persistent tradition insists was—or once had been—a harlot. Leaving this totally unjustified slander unanswered until later, attention must be drawn to the fact that it is this very group which makes it absolutely certain that Jesus was a married man.

The situation must be looked at, not from the point of view of 20th century sexual liberalism, but from that of 1st century Judaism, which permeated and *controlled* the Jew's every action, thought and word. A thing was either sanctioned by the Law or it was not, and what Jesus was doing—if he were unmarried—was a scandal, if nothing more. As he said that he came, not to change but to fulfil the Law of which not one '*yod*' should pass away, it can be taken as certain that he observed not only the letter, but the spirit, of the Law. It is too often forgotten by those who would see Jesus as the sexless, virginal wraith into which doctrine has transformed him, that he preached not continence but chastity and the full honouring of marriage. He wasn't against sex; he was against the unlawful and improper use of it.

However, as he *was* in the intimate company of this group of women—and the Church does not deny it—then we must accept this as a certain guarantee that not only was he married, but that his wife was a member of the party—*which she was!*

The true significance of the marriage at Kana can be seen only after its strange elements have been sifted through the mesh of Jewish social and religious customs applicable to that era. The great non-event begins in *John 2:1-2:*

> And the third day there was a marriage in Kana of Galilee, and the mother of Jesus was there; and both Jesus was called, and his disciples, to the marriage.

Whose marriage was it?

We don't know, because we are not told. Despite the astonishing fact that Jesus' mother is the hostess—thereby making it certain that either the bride or groom was one of her own children—the happy pair is never identified. Why?

Not even when the ruler of the feast—a form of waiter, butler or even caterer—compliments the groom on the wine, does he even open his mouth. Nor, it should be remarked, does he confess that Jesus was the provider. Surely his silence might have been expected to inspire a homily on the subject of man's ingratitude. However, the ruler's praise: 'Thou hast kept the good wine until now' clearly shows that it was the bridegroom's duty to provide the wine. Yet, in the event, not only was it Jesus who supplied it but, equally clearly, his mother Mary expected him to. Why? At what kind of wedding does a guest have this responsibility? Obviously, Jesus must have been something more than a mere guest.

As the story is told, the gospel author leans over backwards to give the impression that this was no more than a humble village function involving only a handful of guests. He names only Jesus and his mother and, without giving names, mentions another twelve which not only included the anonymous bride and groom, but Jesus' brothers as well. The latter information is withheld until the party is returning to Capernaum but it does much more than increase the number of participants by at least five, it adds another bit of evidence that the wedding had involved some member of Jesus' family.

Although no mention is made of Alpheus-Jacob, this is no more than what could be expected in such a whitewash. That it was not a humble village-level function is indicated by the presence of the ruler or caterer and it might well have been a large and 'glittering' feast involving a huge number of guests, and held in some very large house—even a palace—that would have accommodated somewhere about one thousand people.

This figure is justified by the amount of wine allegedly supplied by Jesus through a shoddy 'miracle'.

According to the gospel, he told the servants to fill six wine pots to the brim with water, which he instantly changed to wine. Omitting any comment on the 'miracle' or its likely nature—or even its historicity—our attention is focused on those wine pots whose capacity is given as between 2 and 3 firkins each—a firkin being about 9 Imperial gallons. Averaging their capacity at 2½ firkins, a little arithmetic gives: 6 pots x 2½ firkins x 9 gallons x 8 pints, or 1080 pints . . . which is *equivalent to 90 dozen modern bottles of claret*. Remember that this was an *additional* supply of grog. Not only was it enough to get *sober* guests numbering some seven hundred and fifty rip-roaring drunk, but as many would merely have sipped only for the toasts, there was probably more than enough for a thousand hard drinkers. The image of a humble village wedding is rapidly receding.

How was it that Jesus came to be present at this wedding of a thousand guests and of two people not important enough to be identified, held in a town in the very heart of Hasmonean territory which he had to walk a tough twenty miles uphill to reach?

As the gospel testifies, Jesus was *called* to it—a fact to be remembered—in extremely strange circumstances.

This 'call' was brought to him at Lake Gennesareth by Nathanael of Kana and, though they had never met, they instantly recognised each other. Jesus said to Nathanael: 'When thou wast under the fig tree, I saw thee,' alluding to his habit of taking his ease in his shady garden at Kana. However, his remark points unerringly to the fact that Jesus could have been no stranger to Kana, as Nathanael's next words show by his intant astonishing statement: 'Thou art the King of Israel!' It should be noted that Nathanael did not address Jesus as King of Heaven or by any of the other extravagant euphemisms usually employed by the gospel authors; he gave him the plain, unequivocal title, King of Israel, which is capable of only one meaning, particularly when uttered by a man from Kana, the Hasmonean city.

The implication in the gospel story is that it was Nathanael who brought Jesus the 'call' although this is not expressly stated. The matter is not important for, whether Nathanael brought it or not, Jesus was called. Now this has traditionally been understood to mean that he was *invited* to the wedding when, in fact, he was not! Jesus was called or *summoned* to this wedding, which is a totally different thing.

In those days it was usual for the time of the *'nissu'in'* or formal wedding celebration to be set when the happy pair became betrothed. Having no dates for the days of the year, the Jews reckoned time as so many days before or after some particular religious festival, such as Passover. Being the beginning of Spring, this was a popular time ... as it still is with modern brides, who now call it Easter.

When the future bride and groom lived in the same village there was little hope of him being allowed to forget the fast approaching date. If, however, he had gone to some other town or area to work, or was in the habit of travelling about the countryside—as Jesus did—there was a very real danger that other distractions might cause a lapse of memory, real or assumed. It was therefore the custom to send such a man a 'call'—either orally or in writing—to summon him to present himself by the set date.

In short, the mysterious wedding to which Jesus was called ... was his own!

Now, suddenly, every mysterious piece falls into its correct place in the jig-saw. Now it is only too clear why Mary was acting as hostess and why Jesus provided the wine. When the ruler of the feast congratulated the groom, he praised Jesus, who looked suitably modest and accepted the compliment in gracious silence.

It even explains the huge quantity of wine, for with Jesus the groom and the heir to the Hasmonean throne, it is likely that all the chief men of the Joarib clan and their wives attended. The presence of his brothers is explained as, too, is that of his disciples. It was the custom for the groom to attend with two male witnesses; having only four disciples at that time—twice the number of witnesses required—Jesus might have decided to take all four rather than cause jealousy. However, as the wedding probably occurred many years before he thought of having even one disciple, the men who accompanied him to his wedding were possibly boyhood friends who later became disciples, rather than men who then were.

Most of all, the theory that Jesus was the bridegroom finally and completely explains why the groom in the narrative is anonymous. Needing to report the miracle but embarassed by the explicit revelations of the settings, the author of *John*—or his later editors—solved the problem by deleting all identifying elements conflicting with the, by then, established image of Jesus as the Divine Son of God, who never married and was forever virginal.

The final nail in the coffin of the absurd claim that Jesus had no brothers or sisters is provided by this wedding. It being certain that *one* of Mary's children was involved then, if Jesus were her only child, he must have been the bridegroom.

A final query relates to the locale of the wedding. Why did it take place in Kana of Galilee? Jesus' home town was Nazareth—if it then existed—or Capernaum and the bride certainly came from neither. So, why Kana? It is suggested that the function was held there because it was obligatory for the heir to the Hasmonean throne to be married in the presence of the seniors of the 'family' and Kana, of course, was their feudal base.

And the bride? Who was she?

In view of the evidence put forward in the following chapter, it is difficult not to see her as the woman who appears in the gospels under the threefold identity of the penitent woman, Mary of Bethany and Mary Magdalene, whom the Catholic Church sees as one and the same.

12 / Mary—Harlot or Wife?

It is no accident that Catholic France should possess institutions for rehabilitating prostitutes called 'Les Hospices de la Madeleine', or that the inmates should be known as 'les Madeleines' or Magdalenes.

Thus the slander that Mary called Magdalene had once been a harlot dies hard in the blow-hot, blow-cold world of Catholicism, which once held an entirely different opinion of her. In fact, so highly was she regarded by the early Church that she occupied a position of equal rank and importance with the Virgin. As it is to be doubted that it was her discovery of the empty tomb and being first to speak with the Risen Jesus which, alone, entitled her to this eminence, the suggestion arises that there might have been some other very good reason which, since, has been conveniently forgotten. Venerated, she still is but it is obvious that the 'pecking order' has changed over the centuries. So flimsy is the 'evidence' supporting the calumny that she had been a harlot that the growth of the legend might deliberately have been fostered to distract attention from what, historically, had been this Mary's true position in the life of Jesus.

The scandal—for which there is absolutely no authority or justification anywhere in the New Testament—appears to have been based on differing interpretations of the non-Jewish word 'Magdalene', which might have originated in the name of her reputed village of Migdal, on the Plain of Gennesareth. The truth is that nobody knows, for certain, just what 'Magdalene' meant though some insist that it meant a woman who curled her hair, claimed to be the mark of a harlot in those days. Others point to smoke and see fire in the claim that the Hebrew 'magdalah' and 'megaddeleh' meant, respectively, 'harlot' and 'hairdresser'. Still others identify Mary with the penitent woman who bathed Jesus' feet with her tears of contrition and, still without justification, describe the penitent as a harlot because 'seven devils had been driven out of her'.

Tradition has had it that Mary Magdalene was a wealthy woman; naturally, a snigger has usually accompanied this information. That she was wealthy seems beyond doubt for she was one of that group of women who 'ministered unto him of their substance'; however, there would seem to be a perfectly innocent explanation for her wealth and which might even be the explanation of her 'name'.

Mary's village—whatever its name—has already been mentioned as the place where most of the sacrificial doves used at the Temple were bred, and earned their breeders a vast income. Mary might have been a member of a family engaged in this trade and might even have controlled it, exclusively. This suggestion is based on the fact that 'breeder' in Hebrew is the word *megadal* which, a solution or not, seems just as reasonable as the others so far put forward.

Whatever Mary called Magdalene's trade might have been, the fact that, historically, she was the wife of Jesus—as some traditions insist—would have been sufficient to have earned her the denigration of those determined on the supremacy of the Virgin and the absurd doctrine of the Perpetual Virginity of her son. That she was, indeed, his spouse seems inescapable after a thorough examination of the documents of the faith—not necessarily only those of the New Testament—and the application of some commonsense to their relevant parts.

As presented by the gospels Mary called Magdalene is a figure of mystery in the shadows. Although named early in the story she is ignored until she blazed dramatically onstage at the empty tomb. If one examines the accounts of the Crucifixion and the empty tomb and counts each event as a 'scene', there is a total of eight occasions on which the four gospel authors have an opportunity to name the women present. In a startling six of the eight Mary called Magdalene's name stands at the head of the list, and in all but one she takes precedence over Mary the mother of Jesus.

It is strange that the 4th century editors, who appear to have tampered with so much of the gospel text—and

who were then elevating the Virgin to unimaginable pinna-
cles—should have failed to reverse the listings.

Was the 'pecking order' left as it was because it dare
not be changed? Was it left that way because it was
known exactly *why* the Magdalene had been first on the
list? For example, if she were Jesus' wife and he King of
Israel—if only in the opinion of the Hasmoneans—she
would have taken precedence over his dowager-mother ...
and, clearly, she did!

If we are correct in thinking that all direct references to
the Magdalene as wife have been deleted from the canonical gospels for obvious reasons, then we might expect to
find undeleted references to their true association in some
of the apocryphal gospels, of which there are many. And
we do!

The *Gospel of Mary*, discovered in Egypt in 1896,
leaves little doubt about the matter, suggesting that if they
were not man and wife they should have been. This was
supported by the discovery some fifty years later of fragments of the *Gospel of Philip*, one part of which says:
'There were three who walked with the Lord at all times,
Mary his mother, and her sister (Salome) and Magdalene,
this one who is called his partner.' In the very next sentence the Magdalene is referred to as Jesus' 'spouse'. Later
it describes how Jesus kisses her often and asks the other
women why she doesn't love them as he loves her. Though
these gospels derive from sects having a doctrine different
from Christianity, their early date of the 2nd century suggests that as they were far closer to the events than our
present 4th century gospels they might be more historically accurate.

Whether or not the claim that Jesus and Mary were
man and wife is correct, it is curious to find not a little
circumstantial evidence that he was husband to Mary of
Bethany, whom the Catholic Church holds to have been
identical with Mary called Magdalene. Strangely enough,
this evidence emerges from the least credible of the alleged
miracles performed by Jesus.

Without entering into the argument of the merits or
otherwise of the celebrated 'Raising of Lazarus' as an historical event, we are concerned only with the words and
attitudes of the people concerned; not with the 'miracle' itself.

It will be recalled that Jesus returned to Bethany in response to an urgent summons telling him that Lazarus, the brother of Mary and Martha, was sick unto death and that only Jesus could save him. Instead of rushing home, Jesus mysteriously procrastinates at Caesarea-Phillipi—120 miles away—for 2 days before, finally, setting out. When he arrived at Bethany some 5 or 6 days later, Lazarus had been dead for 4 days so that, as Martha graphically put it: 'Already he stinketh!', and the mourning was well under way.

Hearing that Jesus was making his tardy arrival at last, a furious Martha rushed out of the house and began to upbraid him. 'Lord,' she said, 'If thou hadst been here, my brother had not died!' A long and hardly credible scene followed, during which Mary remained silent inside the house although she, too, was seething. Why didn't she behave as her sister had done? Watch closely what happened next, after Martha returned from giving Jesus 'a piece of her mind'.

> And when she had said, she went her way and called Mary, her sister, secretly saying: The Master is come and calleth thee. As soon as she (Mary) heard that, she arose quickly and came unto him.

Well, there it all is; now it is clear both why Mary had not rushed out but had stayed in the house until called for, and what this has to say about her relationship to Jesus.

In those days a homing husband *sent* for his wife and, until he did so, the little woman sat obediently in her part of the house. This is precisely what Mary of Bethany did! It was not until her sister told her that she had been summoned that Mary 'dropped everything' and rushed out.

Only then did she give Jesus the length of her tongue; significantly, several times she called him 'Baal', which can mean either 'Lord' . . . or 'husband'.

Had the gospels stated explicitly that Mary was Jesus' wife, she could not have been expected to behave in this incident any differently from the way she actually did. If, historically, she were not his wife, then it is extremely curious to find her acting precisely as if she were. Martha, the sister-in-law rushed out; Mary, the wife, sat until summoned!

Perhaps there is another strong hint of their true relationship in *Luke* 10:38-42. Jesus arrived at the house in Bethany and Mary promptly sat at his feet; an intimacy with which all married men are pleasantly familiar. So they sat while Martha was slaving away preparing a meal. Tired of being left to do all the work alone, she complained to Jesus: 'Lord, dost thou not care that my sister hath left me to serve alone? Bid her therefore that she help me!'

Jealousy or not, Martha's direct addressing of Jesus instead of her sister shows as plainly as is possible that Mary was under his control and authority. Had Mary not been married to the man at whose feet she idled, Martha would have done exactly as she would had Jesus not been present; she would have attacked her sister directly for sloth.

So it is this small and very human episode that might easily be of great importance in determining the true relationship of Mary of Bethany to Jesus which, on the evidence, certainly appears to have been that of wife. That this Mary was identical with Mary called Magdalene must remain inconclusive and only a suspicion, though the latter's post-resurrectional scene with Jesus—during which she addresses him as Lord or husband—seems to suggest that she, too, was his wife. It is these things, then, which tend to merge the two Marys into one, perhaps correctly.

Perhaps the 'fifteenth' scroll written by Jesus of Gennesareth—which certainly makes it plain that he had been married—contains the name of his wife, which might eventually prove to have been ... Mary Magdalene, as those apocryphal gospels claim.

Now arises the question: if Jesus were married at any stage in his life, was there any issue? The other Jesus claimed at least one son. Is there any indication in the gospels that the Jesus of Christian imagery also fathered a son?

Although we postpone full discussion of the probability until the next chapter, it can be anticipated by stating that the gospels—and tradition—give an affirmative to the question. Events help foster the hypothesis.

Turning back to the time when it is thought that the wedding in Kana occurred—some twenty years before the gospel time setting—we read that immediately that function was over, Jesus, his mother, brothers, and disciples returned to Capernaum. A few days later, apparently alone, Jesus left on his journey to Jerusalem and the Passover.

Before another had come around, and at the time of a festival thought to have been the Feast of the Dedication—held in December and therefore at a most eloquent interval of ten months in those pre-Pill times—we find Jesus again in Kana of Galilee, apparently for no particular reason; certainly, none is given.

Why was he there?

If, as is claimed, he was married in Kana because Hasmonean tradition required that the heir be married in the presence of the clan, is it not conceivable that he might have been obliged to make another journey there to present the very same people the fruit of that marriage ... the seed of his loins and his heir?

13 / A Sunday Stroll in the Temple

To this point it is still possible for those whose eyes are still atwinkle with stardust to accept the portrait of Jesus painted by the gospels, but surely the illusion must be shattered for all but the most stubborn and stiffnecked by the events of what is called Palm Sunday and the seven days following.

The choice is between the historical and the theological Jesus. Are we to accept as historically true or even likely, the man apparently aimlessly wandering to and fro and backwards and forwards on a dream-like 'mission' which had no observable object but the calling of sinners to repentance? Alternatively, we are more entitled to see the historical Jesus as a rebel-rousing claimant to the Hasmonean throne of Israel *pretending* to be 'as harmless as a dove' but, all the time, covertly preaching rebellion in whatever village, town or city that had 'ears to hear'?

Clearly, whatever the nature of Jesus' 'mission', the crunch came on Palm Sunday, pallidly described by the author of the gospel of *Mark*—or his editors—in the following unreal terms:

> And they came to Jerusalem: and Jesus went into the Temple and began to cast out them that sold and bought in the Temple, and overthrew the tables of the money-changers, and the seats of them that sold doves.

In view of the background of events so far painted, is that a likely version of what really happened that day? Compared with the accounts of the delirious reaction of the crowds as Jesus made his triumphant entry into the Holy City, it stands as a deliberate write down and an attempt to minimise what must have been, at the very least, a riot and almost certainly was a great deal more than that.

Curiously enough, it was only about a week before this event that Jesus' apparent lethargy vanished. Once he decided to act on the message that Mary's brother, Lazarus, was 'sick unto death'—possibly a signal with a totally different significance—everything became bustling action. Suddenly, the sequence of events starts racing madly, as in a film run at breakneck speed.

In a matter of two weeks he received that vital signal from Bethany, walked one hundred and twenty miles back to there, raised Lazarus from the 'dead', incurred the full enmity of the Sanhedrin for the first time, 'rejected' an appeal to declare himself King of Israel but entered Jerusalem *like* a King and drove the money-changers from the Temple, ate his Last Supper and was 'betrayed' by Judas, submitted like a lamb to arrest for no discernible reason and was tried, convicted, crucified, dead, buried and risen . . . all in fourteen days!

What is likely to have motivated all this sudden activity?

It seems almost as if, while Jesus and his disciples were in hiding up north, somebody south in Jerusalem was busy setting the stage for the big events that were to come. Was the message about Lazarus merely a signal of recall, telling him that all was ready? Ready for what? Was it a case of now or never if Jesus were ever to make his successful bid for the throne?

The key event in the rapidfire fourteen days of action was undoubtedly his entry into Jerusalem and the 'cleansing of the Temple', which has overtones of Judas Maccabeus' similar act back in the days of the Assyrian overlords. The true nature of what the 'cleansing' was all about must be filtered out of what we are told, which is unlikely to have been the historical facts. The very nature of Roman discipline was such that it was impossible for the event to have been little more than the schoolboy prank it is suggested to have been, or for it to have stopped there. Even modest brawls in the Temple area brought violent Roman reaction, and it is believed that the 'cleansing' was not only no exception, but brought savage retribution on those responsible.

Consider the timing of the event. It was less than a week before the Passover, which the Romans always considered a tinder dry period when anything could, and did, happen. The Jews flocked in their *millions* to attend this

Holy Festival, for every healthy male over the age of 12 living within ninety miles of the Temple was compelled by the Law to attend his God and give an account of himself. Indeed, a Roman estimate of the Jews attending the Passover of very close to three million, which shows that the Jews packed a powerful 'punch' into a relatively small area.

It was at Passover then, when religious and nationalistic fervour ran high and hot, that trouble would start . . . if it were ever to start. What made the Roman apprehension all the greater was that the milling multitude included tens of thousands of the rough, tough Galileans who were mostly Zealots and ardent Messianists. Expected to control the myriads was a force consisting of the Jewish Temple Police—amounting to no more than a probable two hundred—and one cohort of Roman troops, normally five hundred men. No wonder that when Governor Pontius Pilate made his customary Passover visit from his palace in Caesarea, he brought another cohort of seasoned troops to stiffen the Temple Guard in the riot season. He, however, would not arrive before the middle of the week, as would Herod Antipas, with an additional cohort. So that the position was that on Palm Sunday there were only one third of the troops who would be on deck later in the week, and so if any attempt to take over the Temple and the City were to succeed, it was a plain case of now or never.

It seems obvious that, for Jesus, it was *now!* So, all being ready and the Passover less than a week away, the plan started to unroll.

That weekend there was a ceremony at Bethany, only a faint echo of which can still be detected in the gospels. That it was of great significance is surely indicated by the fact that Jesus was anointed, and it is the implications of this which enable us to detect the true nature of the proceedings. These began with the serving of an important meal, which might have been of great symbolic significance and which was attended by all the disciples. It is also possible that the party included important Hasmoneans who would lead the Zealot 'troops' on the Sunday. While their attendance might be explained on the score of a need for a 'pre-battle' briefing, it can better be justified by the fact of Jesus' anointment.

That this must have been of an entirely different nature

than the gospels suggest, is shown by a tiny but astonishing clue overlooked by the usually gimlet-eyed editors intent on deleting embarrassing and telltale details. While they have succeeded in distorting the image of the holy ritual the ceremony must have been, they have utterly failed to realise the significance of the substance with which Jesus was anointed . . . and by whom it was used.

In the accounts given us, Jesus was anointed by Mary of Bethany who, we say, was his wife and Mary called Magdalene under another name. Now what was there in the fact that Mary anointed Jesus that was worth reporting? Had she merely poured olive oil on his head and feet, this would have been no more than a frequent wifely duty and, as such, utterly unimportant information. However, the unguent used wasn't olive oil . . . but 'spikenard'.

Not only was 'spikenard' terribly expensive—as is borne out by the sordid, alleged quarrel between Mary and Judas—but its manufacture and even possession was severely restricted; its use was strictly reserved, by the Law, to the holy anointing of Irael's Kings!

This makes it absolutely certain that however humble and primitive might have been the ceremony—and it was probably no more than symbolic—its significance was both political and religious. As an added bonus to this information, the fact that it was Mary who anointed Jesus proves beyond all doubt that she was his wife for, so strictly observed were the regulations governing the use of 'spikenard' that she would not have dared have it in her hand unless she was the wife of a Royal personage!

It seems obvious that the gospel authors were a mite sensitive about the ceremony. Luke doesn't report it at all; Matthew and Mark have an anonymous woman anoint Jesus' feet, while only John describes its true implications by reporting both the use of 'spikenard' and Mary as the anointer. Both other authors who mention the ceremony at all defeat themselves by trying to be a little too clever; they describe the unguent as 'ointment', which is merely a truncated form of 'oil of anointment' which, of course, was the Royal 'spikenard'.

The fact that this symbolic politico-religious ceremony was held at Bethany on the Saturday night preceding Palm Sunday and the great event that was to happen, gives immense significance to both, and makes it quite certain that the alleged 'cleansing' of the Temple was Jesus' bid to capture Jerusalem and restore the Hasmonean Throne. Assuming this to be so, how good were his chances? As it happened—and on paper—his chances were excellent and all systems go.

There are conflicting reports as to the number of Jesus' armed supporters. One tradition claims their number as high as four thousand, while a lost work by Josephus, of which we have a medieval Hebrew copy, puts their total at two thousand. On the other hand, the Roman Procurator of Phoenicia, Arabia Libanitis and Bithynia—Sossianus Hierocles—a notorious 1st century persecutor of Christians, says that Jesus led a band of 'highway robbers' numbering more than nine hundred men. Whatever the truthful figure it seems quite certain that Jesus had a considerable armed force with him in the vicinity of Bethany and the Mount of Olives.

In addition, a popular uprising in favour of the Hasmoneans would undoubtedly involve every last Galilean Zealot in and around Jerusalem. Against these formidable forces Rome could muster a mere five hundred troops while the Temple Police, responsible to the Sanhedrin, numbered only two hundred but, as their job was only to protect the Temple, Rome couldn't expect their assistance in troubles elsewhere in the City. With the odds against them a minimum of eight to one, not even the valiant Legionaries could be expected to prevail. So—on paper— it looked as though Pilatus and Antipas, when they arrived in a few days time, would be too late; instead of the sullen crowds which were their usual lot, they would be met by Jerusalem's barred gates and a derisive mob of Zealots manning the City's high battlements.

Only . . . it didn't quite work out that way. The rebellion was a dismal failure and, for this, Jesus had only his popularity to blame.

The beginnings of the attempted coup are described in the gospels so that there is no great need of speculation. Leaving the house in Bethany with only a few disciples so as to arouse no suspicion in the watching Sanhedrin spies, Jesus moved across the crown of the Mount of Olives and began to descend, gathering his Zealot supporters on the way. But then he made a fatal error which doomed the whole venture.

Seeing an ass tethered outside a village on the slope, he

sent a couple of disciples to borrow it, thinking no doubt, to inject a little drama into things by becoming the living prophecy of *Zecharia* 9:9 which says: 'Rejoice greatly, O Daughter of Zion; shut O daughter of Jerusalem: Behold, thy King cometh unto thee . . . meek . . . and riding upon an ass . . . !' What Jesus failed to realise, however, was that Jerusalem's inflated population knew its Prophets as well as he, for it promptly took him at face value and, as he trotted towards the Golden Gate, which then led directly into the Temple area, an almighty shout of joy rent the air. Tearing fronds from the date-palms which then grew profusely in the King's Garden in the Kidron Valley, they strewed them in his path. Shouting his name and imploring him to rise and save them from Rome—as their King and Messiah surely would—their acclamations became one mighty, thunderous roar.

No doubt apprehensive that the Guards would have been alerted, Jesus must have had a moment of indecision about the wisdom of proceeding with his plan but now, literally, there was no going back; the vast crowd pressed hundreds thick behind . . . and the only way to go was ahead.

Flanked by an escort of brawny Galileans who were seeing prophecy made manifest and history created, Jesus trotted into the 'Court of the Gentiles' where the real action was to begin. Here it was that the money-changers set up their tables to fleece the faithful and rob the poor, and these were to provide the 'excuse' for the riot which was to be used as a cover for the serious business of capturing the City. Ignoring the white, scared faces of the startled Temple Police of the Levites Jesus slipped off the ass and gave the signal to his henchmen. From beneath their cloaks they all produced knotted whips and cudgels and set to their work.

In a flash, all was confusion. Over went the money-lenders' tables, sending the delighted urchins diving for the glittering golden cascades of coins whose outraged owners' shrill imprecations quickly changed to screams of pain as the flailing whips lashed at their writhing bodies. So far so good, Jesus must have thought. The riot had got away to an excellent start and now could only spread.

Alas for the grand plan. The Captain of the Temple Police blew a shrill blast on his whistle and down the steps of the Antonia Fortress adjoining the Temple descended an avalanche of steel as five hundred Roman Legionaries fell upon the mob. Hemmed in as they were by the terrified crowd which Jesus' grand-standing had generated, the Zealots had no room to swing their swords; all they could do was drop them as inconspicuously as possible and try to escape in the confusion. As we know from the gospels, not all of them made it.

Bruised and bleeding, the survivors struggled from the City and back to the safety of the Mount of Olives and Bethany, where Jesus and his lieutenants got their breath and counted up the cost as best they could. In dribs and drabs more groaning men painfully climbed the hill ... and then the track up from the Temple was empty.

Speculative though most of the foregoing is, it is no more than 'meat' put upon the bare bones of the gospel accounts of the events of Palm Sunday which, as they stand in those documents, are divorced from the likely reality. What really happened that day *must* have included the savage retribution of the Romans and to pretend that it did not is nonsense.

This view is supported by all four gospels, of which *Mark* 15:7 is the most explanatory: 'And there was one named Barabbas, which lay bound with them that had made insurrection with him, who had committed murder in the insurrection.' *Matthew* calls this Barabbas a 'notable' man but fails to indicate why.

Insurrection, of course, is an uprising against the ruling authority which, we say, is precisely what Jesus did or tried to do that day, as his foolish act of riding that ass demonstrates. While it *might* have been some other insurrection which Barabbas was involved in, this hardly seems likely for the inference points to an event in the immediate past and, when Barabbas comes into the story, Jesus' insurrection was only five days past. Also please to note that other prisoners lay bound or fettered with this man Barabbas, which brings up a curious point.

The Romans in Palestine (Judea) kept no prisons for the way their justice worked made them entirely superfluous. If a man were innocent he was freed with a hobnailed boot in the backside; if guilty he was either put to productive slavery or, in the event that his crime were capital, executed. Yet, despite the summary nature of their justice, here was Barabbas and an untold number of other prisoners still awaiting execution a possible five days later.

Why, is a very interesting question with an astonishing answer which, however, must wait upon other things.

Had Jesus' venture not been a major attack—had he been accompanied by only a handful of disciples—he would never have got away from the 'Court of the Gentiles' for he would probably have been cut down on the spot. As he wasn't, there must have been a considerable force protecting him at the Temple and, later, at Bethany. As he was well known and both the Romans and the Sanhedrin maintained a large spy ring, it is quite impossible for the authorities to have been unaware of his base of operations and refuge, yet no move was made to arrest him.

Why was this insurrectionist allowed to stay free for at least four days when, historically, even such a minor disturbance which the gospels admit to, would have resulted in his immediate arrest, and possibly worse? Were the authorities afraid to tackle his Zealot supporters? It looks suspiciously like it and, of course, strengthens the tradition that these were numbered in their thousands. With most of them camped on and around the Mount of Olives the Romans would have had little chance of capturing their quarry or of even getting back to the city alive.

Assuming that this might have been the true position, the next intriguing question is why Jesus hung around at Bethany when he could have escaped in virtually any direction—with no man to say him nay—and ended the stalemate by meekly turning himself in?

Here again our only recourse is to speculation but it is only fair to qualify this by saying that it is not entirely so; there being some very solid 'bones' of evidence spread through the mixture.

A likely hypothesis of what happened at Bethany after the last straggler came limping and groaning up the hill is largely based on later events which might here be mentioned only briefly because they will be discussed fully as the story unfolds. Though imaginative, the following is not at all unlikely.

As that Sunday faded with the setting sun there must have been many women in the village who stood on the brow of the hill peering hopefully down into the thickening darkness of the Kidron Valley looking for one who was yet to return; among them, perhaps, was Mary of Bethany ... and even a man or two such as the disciple Simon the Zealot, father of Julas the Sicarii. Perhaps even Jesus was there, too, as anxious as his wife for sight or sound that would tell them that their firstborn son was safe after all; the 20 year old Jesus who, to avoid confusion with his father's name, was usually called 'bar Abbas' or 'son of the Master'.

The suggestion is not as fantastic as it might seem to some, for no less an authority than the great scholar and Father of the early Church, Jerome—writing in the 4th century A.D.—says that in the long lost 'Gospel of the Hebrews' the given name of this man Bar Abbas was ... Jesus. Indeed, the original text of *Matthew* 27:16-17 certainly once contained this name though, like much else, it has since vanished.

Some scholars say that it was deleted by pious editors in order to preserve the sanctity which, by then, had come to surround the name 'Jesus'. Well, perhaps so ... although one would not need to be unduly suspicious to imagine that the editorial pencil had really been drawn through the prisoner's given name, and 'bar Abbas' made into 'Barabbas' in order to conceal an embarrassing fact of history.

That the man's given name was Jesus is made plain by Jerome's use of the phrase—taken directly from the 'Gospel of the Hebrews'—*'filius magistri eorum'*, which translates from the Latin into 'the son of their teacher or master'. Additional corroborative evidence that the notable prisoner's name was 'Jesus bar Abbas' is provided by some cursive gospel manuscripts and by the Armenian and Jerusalem Syriac versions of the gospel of *Matthew* ... *and these are still to be seen.*

The first night of anguish passed and Monday was a torture. Jerusalem buzzed. Rumours sped from lying lip to avid ear. Pilate was making a forced march to arrive a day earlier than planned; Herod Antipas would be here with five thousand troops within the hour ... and so on from one lie to a greater. The Temple area was an armed camp and to Hades with the Law of the Jews. Roman Legionaries and Temple Police were everywhere. Heavily disguised spies heard their whispers and rushed them back to the Sanhedrin. Other spies collected the few crumbs of gossip for news of Judas, bar Abbas, and the others and took them back to grieving Bethany. But news, there was not ... until late that afternoon, miraculously, up the hill came an unharmed Judas the Sicarii!

Now there was news, but of the worst kind!

Captured by the Temple Police on Sunday, he had been taken before the high priest, Caiaphas, and questioned, threatened and beaten. True to his Zealot oath he had endured his scourging with silent fortitude until it was interrupted by the arrival of a centurion from the Antonia bringing the news that one of the other captives was the insurrection leader's son, Jesus bar Abbas.

The information gave the High Priest a glimmer of hope to lighten the darkness of his fear. If he used his wits, he could appease the anger of Pilatus and Herod Antipas when they arrived breathing bloody vengeance on the Jews. Only the other day in the Sanhedrin he had joined in the argument about Jesus the Galilean and the threat his activities posed to the population of Jerusalem. His solution? The same as Gamaliel's, that it was expedient that this one man should be done away with rather than that many should die in the certain Roman reprisals that would follow his uprising. Well, they hadn't taken his advice ... and now look at the mess they were in. But at least they had the Hasmonean's son ... and if the centurion would take the advice being cunningly whispered in his ear—and this coin bag jingling at his belt—perhaps they could get this ridiculous king, himself. We've got the cub; let us not try for the lion!

'You, Judas the Sicarii, tell us how to trap your leader without a fight and we will pay you well!' The centurion looked meaningly at the High Priest who tossed the black, kidskin bag of silver coins at the Zealot's feet. The tough Sicarii picked it up and sent it crashing so hard against the wall that it burst and spilled the contents on the floor. Judas counted them where they lay, shining. Exactly thirty!

The centurion was as tough as Judas.

'So much for money,' he shouted. 'Now hear me well, you dog. Get you to your leader and tell him that we have his cub, Jesus bar Abbas, who was seen to commit murder on a Roman soldier in the "Court of the Gentiles". Thus he will surely die when Pilatus arrives unless ... unless his life is bought by his father! Go tell this impudent "king" of yours that, as he'll eventually be taken and crucified, he might as well save his son's life by surrendering. Go now and tell him what Rome has said!'

Impossible? Fantastic? Why? Merely because it is contrary to the story learned at Sunday school?

There is no escaping the fact that Jesus bar Abbas *was* the son of Jesus and Mary of Bethany, called Magdalene. There is no doubt that he was a Roman prisoner captured in an insurrection in which he had committed murder. There's no question but that he was a 'notable' prisoner which, as son of the pretender to the Hasmonean Throne, he undeniably would have been. And the gospels themselves attest to the fact that he was released, or that a 'swap' was made under incredible circumstances. Jesus bar Abbas was released for Jesus his father by a device invented by either the gospel authors or their editors, which claimed that the Jews had a custom whereby a prisoner of their choice was released at *Passover*. History knows of no such custom nor, even more significantly, do the writings of the Jews ... which fill an enormous number of highly detailed volumes. Lastly, but not least, such a kindly indulgence would never have been granted by any Roman Governor, who had to refer his almost every decision back to Rome for Imperial ratification.

Isn't it possible in the circumstances that the celebrated 'swap' incident at the trial of Jesus is but a distorted echo of the bargaining that might have gone on behind the walls of the High Priest's house or of Pontius Pilate's palace?

With the choice between father and son, it is difficult not to see the next scene in the drama as one deliberately planned by Jesus to save his beloved son and heir from death on the Cross ... and to preserve the line of the Hasmoneans.

If a certain archaeologist named 'Grosset' is correct in seeing Jesus as identical with Jesus of Gennesareth, the author of the 'fifteenth scroll''—whose son was crucified by the Romans at Masada some time after 66 A.D.—then, for Jesus bar Abbas the respite was only temporary. Rome got him in the end ... as it did all the Hasmoneans!

14 / That Strange Last Supper

Christian doctrine asserts that Jesus went to the Cross in order to redeem Mankind, offering himself as a living sacrifice for its sins. Is this true in the context of history, or is it rather a statement of theological belief that is 'held to be true' and thus more sophist than real?

Careful examination of the alleged utterances of Jesus show that the only kind of redemption in his mind applied specifically and exclusively to the people of tiny Judea. The Jews were God's chosen who, by permitting themselves to be ruled by pagans and meekly accepting their fate, had deeply sinned for they had broken their covenant with God. Redemption could come only by a shattering of the *status quo*, which required the arising of a Messiah-King to lead them from the darkness of their sinful acceptance of the situation, into the loving sunshine of a placated God. Put in blunt terms, redemption meant a revolt against the Romans.

Again from the gospels, it is clear that Jesus must have had a long set date for his uprising and that the closer he moved towards it, the broader and more frequent became his hints that the revolt might fail.

His constant harping, towards the end, that he was destined to go to the Cross has been claimed by the Church as an example of his Divine Prescience and his awareness of his role as the Son of God when, in fact, it could have been due to a perfectly normal apprehension about his predictable future. He did not need to be very prescient to know that crucifixion was the fate of any rebel leader who failed, as they all did; he had too many awful examples within the Hasmonean family to be under any illusion about that!

That he represents the perfect picture of a man swept along by a tide of events he is powerless to prevent, is a much more likely image of the historical man than that put forward by the gospels which, after all, are doctrinal works rather than historical.

Jesus knew perfectly well that he might fail, yet destiny demanded that he make his bid for the Royal restoration despite its inevitable cost. However, we say, he hadn't calculated that his own son and heir's life would be part of that cost.

Having failed, there he was in Bethany surrounded by a strong armed force which the Romans were afraid to tackle, with all his escape options open and free as the air to go wherever he wished yet, after several days of procrastination, he apparently gave himself up, voluntarily. Why?

Theology claims to know why, and its answer is Christianity, which represents no more than one tiny sect's speculations about where it stood in relation to God. Being so, this answer can only be considered more philosophical than historical and can therefore be as impossibly wrong as it is claimed to be possibly right.

Having found Jesus' apparently senseless decision to surrender entirely motiveless, Christianity—in the guise of St. Paul—sought for one in the supernatural when, all the time, the motive was chained to a wall in the yard of the Antonia Fortress, hard by the Temple of God in Jerusalem.

It is not claimed that this thesis is correct, but merely that it could be and, on such evidence as has been produced—mostly from the gospels—that it might be. It is on these terms, then, that we proceed.

The dilemma in which Jesus found himself after his son, Jesus bar Abbas, was captured had a perfectly simple solution. Having, himself, failed at his try to restore the Hasmonean monarchy did not necessarily mean that his son would, when his turn came. The vital thing was that he must make the attempt and to do that, he must live!

After almost two days of listening to this advice and that, and knowing that when it came to the crunch he had no choice, Jesus decided to accept the Roman offer to exchange his son for him. It is suggested that he decided to announce his decision to his disciples and the chief men of the Hasmonean Zealots at what is called the Last Supper. The exact nature and significance of this famous meal has been the cause of bitter wrangling from the earliest days of the Church and, even today, this has been more ac-

cepted than explained. The dispute arose from the odd
fact that the first three gospels disagree with *John* on not
only what kind of meal it was, but also when it was held.

The authors of the first three gospels—called the Synoptics, because they tell roughly the same story—see the
meal as the orthodox Jewish Paschal Feast, eaten the moment the silver trumpets on the Temple walls announced
the beginning of the Passover, and that it was served the
night before Jesus' surrender, trial and crucifixion. Such a
chronology is utterly impossible because it requires that
Jesus was crucified on what was not only the orthodox
Sabbath but, this year, also the Passover and therefore
doubly sacred.

Not only was it forbidden by God that anyone crucified
should be permitted to hang on the cross for as much as
even one minute into the Sabbath—a Jewish law scrupu-
lously observed by the Romans—but the Synoptics contra-
dict themselves later, and support the gospel of *John*
which states that Jesus was removed from the Cross *because the Sabbath was fast approaching!*

Using Christian day names to avoid confusion—and
keeping in mind that Jewish 'days' both begin and end at
sunset—this meant that Friday was about to become Saturday. It also meant that, according to the Synoptics,
Jesus had eaten the Passover on our Thursday night; an
impossible act for any orthodox Jew!

If Jesus had already eaten the Passover when he went
to the Cross on Friday, he could have done so only because of a commitment to the Essenes, whose Sabbath and
Passover fell a full two days ahead of the Temple, beginning on Wednesday instead of Friday night.

Observing the solar calendar, in opposition to the lunar
followed by the Temple, the Essenes held it absurd to talk
about days and nights until God created the stars of the
firmament—which, according to *Genesis* 1:14-19, he did
on the fourth day of the week. Thus, instead of the orthodox Saturday Sabbath, the Essene's Sabbath fell on
Wednesday. Another peculiarity of their calendar was
that, unlike orthodoxy—whose Passover could fall on any
day in the week—the Essenic Passover always fell on the
same Wednesday Sabbath every year.

Just what Jesus was doing in the company of the
Jerusalem sectarians on the night of the sacred Paschal
Feast instead of in the bosom of his own family—as might

have been expected on what he clearly assumed was to be his last Passover—is a question tossed to all those Christians who insist on the originality of their faith. They would do well to read something of the sect's doctrine, ritual and liturgy in some of the almost two thousand volumes of learned analysis spawned by the Dead Sea Scrolls; they might be astonished at the sect's amazing parallelisms with their own 'unique' faith.

The gospel of *John* does not claim that what has become known as the Last Supper—surely a deliberately obfuscating name—was the Passover, Essenic or otherwise. The fact that it anticipated the orthodox Passover makes it almost certain that it was the sacred feast of the Essenes. One of the most significant pieces of supporting evidence is that, while the Passover of orthodox Judaism was essentially a *family* feast attended by both women and children, as well as the menfolk, the Essenic Passover was strictly for men only ... which is precisely how all four gospels describe the meal eaten by Jesus.

Whatever its true nature and significance, there were certain curious features about the meal's organisation and locale that are not without interest, and might even be of great importance.

Among the intriguing questions is why Jesus, allegedly being sought by the authorities for the insurrection of the previous (Palm) Sunday in the Temple, should have elected to quit the security of Bethany to put his head in the 'oven' of a Jerusalem stiff with spies and informers? Less than one hundred yards away from the chosen house of the Upper Room was that of the High Priest, Caiaphas, who had already expounded to the Sanhedrin that it was expedient that Jesus should die rather than that all Jews should feel the rage of Rome. If the compelling reason were not to eat the Passover of the Essenes, it is difficult to see any other. Perhaps a clue lies in the house chosen for the Feast's setting ... and in its selection.

Two disciples were sent from Bethany to Jerusalem with instructions to locate and follow a man carrying a water-pitcher, entering the same house that he would enter, there to arrange to eat the Passover.

That something clandestine was in the air seems obvious from the reek of cloak-and-dagger in the instructions. Jerusalem was a mile-square city; where, in its millions, were they to find this oddity of a man carrying a water-pitcher, and thus doing a woman's work? Such a man would have been laughed off the streets . . . unless his dress proclaimed that he belonged to a womanless household, and had to do his own fetching and carrying. The only persons known to have qualified were the Essenes, who wore a distinctive white habit and who had settled in large numbers in an area of the south-western corner of the Upper City. In fact, so numerous were they that a city gate at this spot was called 'The Gate of the Essenes'. Beside it was the Lower Pool of Gihon, to which the women flocked to fill their waterpots. Here, in all probability, the two disciples began their vigil. Finally picking up their man, Peter and John Zebedee followed him through the narrow, winding streets and alleys, and slipped furtively into the house after him.

Now, a question about this house. If, as some claim, it is built upon the foundations of the original, why did Jesus need an Upper Room measuring about 60 x 30 feet—space for at least a couple of hundred people—to accommodate a mere thirteen? Add to this incongruity the odd fact that the Last Supper was held in Jerusalem at all, and everything points to the fact that a large room was chosen because a large assembly was expected! Who, apart from the Essenes, are these others likely to have been and why were they being brought together at this particular time?

In the circumstances it is extremely difficult not to see them as leaders and commanders of the various Zealot-Hasmonean groups who were Jesus' supporters and financial backers. Then, as now, political candidates needed funds and even the most enthusiastic guerilla army needs to be paid. Even had they been paid at the then going rate for a day labourer of one Roman denarius (10 cents), the armed forces alleged by Josephus to have been camped on the Mount of Olives in support of Jesus—two thousand men—would have cost $200 per day, and they are likely to have been paid at least double the rate for a labourer. At a minimum they would have cost $60,000 in a full year, and possibly twice this then-huge amount. This money had to come from somewhere and it is likely that other wealthy men shared the burden with Joseph of Arimathea.

At the feast in the Upper Room, there was probably a hot argument about the previous Sunday's debacle and the arrest of Jesus bar Abbas and others. However excitedly the argument might have waxed, undoubtedly the solution must have been left to Jesus and, as we know, it was to turn himself in. Perhaps, as the assembly broke up, farewells were said and promises obtained of support for Jesus bar Abbas when his turn should come to make a bid for the Throne of the Hasmoneans. There might even have been a grim jest tossed about that, if God were kind, they might all meet one day on 'Galilee', which was the popular name for the Mount of Olives owing to its frequent occupancy by the Galilean Zealots.

Finally the door of the upper room closed on the last of them and Jesus was left alone with his twelve disciples . . . and Joseph of Arimathea. It was then that Jesus and the others really got down to business.

Few men, when trapped and cornered, chuck in the towel without making a desperate fight for their lives and, we imagine, Jesus was no exception.

Knowing what would happen to him the moment the Romans got him in exchange for his son—that he'd be up on the cross before one could say 'Yohan Rubensohn'—Jesus and his aides put their heads together to evolve some plan by which the cross might yet be cheated of its victim.

Certainly Jesus had to go to the cross . . . but did he necessarily have to die on it?

If the inevitable march of events couldn't be prevented, perhaps they could be controlled in such a way that there was a slim chance of survival.

As will be shown, Jesus—or someone near to him—did, in fact, control those events.

15 / The Plan to Cheat the Cross

Strange though it may seem, crucifixion was not invariably fatal!

The garrulous Josephus records that during the siege of Jerusalem by the Romans in 66 A.D., he came across three friends of his, each nailed to his friendly neighbourhood cross by the roadside. Having gone over to the enemy when the defence—which he conducted—of the Hasmonean city of Jotapata collapsed, history's first known 'quisling' found it an easy matter to prevail upon General Titus to spare their lives by taking them down from their crosses. Though two of them died—having already been three days 'on the nails'—the third recovered and lived to boast, no doubt, of how he had cheated the cross.

What is significant about this story is that not only did that unknown man survive crucifixion but, in doing so, experienced a very special form of Jewish resurrection, having gone right to the open door of death ... and returned.

Differently expressed and with heavy emphasis on the supernatural, this is precisely what the gospels relate about Jesus.

Although it is not suggested that the Josephus incident inspired the gospel authors—whose writings were certainly published after 66 A.D.—who can say positively that it did not? However that might have been, the story is repeated merely to prove the point that crucifixion was not always fatal, and that this depended on both the method chosen and the time the victim had been on the cross. These were the two vital factors which were open to influence and control and which option Jesus decided to exercise.

It is suggested that he did this by strictly controlling the 'clock'.

At about our time of 9 p.m. that night the Orthodox

Passover was only 45 hours away and it was in this fact that Jesus' hope lay. The Jewish Law that no crucified man or his body should be permitted to remain on the cross into the Sabbath meant that if Jesus were crucified between now and sunset on Friday, he must be removed from the cross before that time, dead or alive! Thus he had 45 hours in which to exchange himself for his son, stand trial and face the inevitable penalty, and to cheat the cross and Rome, although giving the appearance of having allowed the law to run its course.

Although 45 hours might seem little enough to a man facing death, it was actually far more time than Jesus needed if the exquisitely timed plan were to succeed. Somehow or other, he must draw out the proceedings of his surrender and trial so that he would not go to the cross before some time on Friday morning. Any earlier and he might have to spend so many hours in agony that death would be certain; any later and Pilate might defer the execution until after the Sabbath . . . with the same, but more certain, result.

As the two methods of Roman execution by crucifixion have been fully described in the introduction to this work, no recapitulation is necessary, except to remind the forgetful that each was designed so that a victim could spend up to nearly seven days on the cross—if he survived that long—or less than one day. Somehow or other Jesus must time events so that the latter method was chosen by the Romans. Just how to do this must have been the subject of spirited debate around the suppertable that night in the upper room.

These were all Galileans and few in Judea knew as much about crucifixion as they, having seen up to two thousand of their countrymen crucified at one time. Even in those days there were men who, as the modern idiom puts it, 'knew the lurks'. One such might be that anyone spending only a few hours bound to the cross instead of being nailed, might contrive to give the appearance of death to the executioner by taking a drug administered by his friends. Possibly a little bribery would ensure that the executioner wouldn't examine the 'dead' man too closely. After all, Roman soldiers were only human. Nauseated by the constant slaughter which had none of the excitement of battle, an executioner might readily accept a handful of gold to accept a feigned death as actual, and cut down a victim for his friends to carry away and 'bury'.

Nor was there any shortage of drugs to give the pretence of death. To the north of Judea lay all of Asia Minor, the traditional growing-ground of the delightful '*papaver somniferum*' . . . the *opium* poppy.

In addition to this sophisticated drug, Judea itself produced another which was common to all grain growing countries which suffered late, wet harvests—'*claviceps purperea*'—or, as we know it, Ergot, a fungus which produces Lysergic Acid—L.S.D.!

As raw, unmilled grain is hardly the ideal diet for hungry men, the gospel account of Jesus and his disciples plucking ears of wheat to assuage their hunger takes on an interesting overtone. In view of the almost general experience of modern users of L.S.D. who report having had intense religious experiences, including heavenly visions and even of talking with God, one recalls the equally strange heavenly visions of Israel's ancient Prophets. Were these, too, induced by nibbling at grain infested with the Lysergic-laced fungus?

Leaving this interesting speculation to see what answers, if any, the group in the upper room might have found to the problem of how any selected drug might be introduced to a man on the cross, we find that a solution was found . . . as the gospels themselves report.

At the crucifixion, when Jesus complained of thirst, he was offered a sponge soaked in vinegar and gall. Refusing this, he later apparently accepted it and, almost immediately after, 'died'.

'Vinegar', of course, was merely sour red wine—with a high alcohol content—but what else should 'gall' happen to be but the derivative of the pretty '*papaver somniferum*' or opium!

Curiously enough, most of the argument that has gone on about this incident of the 'sponge-on-the-reed' has been devoted to the reed; what was on the sponge has apparently been ignored.

Matthew and *Mark* call whatever it was on which the saturated sponge was proffered to Jesus a 'reed' and let it go at that; *Luke* doesn't record how the 'vinegar' was offered, merely that it was, while *John* says that the sponge was put on the end of a '*hyssop*'.

Now, the '*hyssop*' was a thin and scrawny hollow

stemmed plant of no great length or strength; a twig of it would undoubtedly have buckled under the heavy weight of a saturated sponge speared on to its tip. By an odd chance, 'speared' might be the very word to provide the clue to the truth of the gospel-legend that a soldier had pierced Jesus' side in order to test whether he was really dead or merely pretending to be.

The Roman guard at the Cross carried full military equipment, which included the fearsome javelin or spear called *'hanith'* in Hebrew. However, the same language has a similar word, *'kaneth'*, which means 'reed', as also does *'kana'*, to which the Hasmonean town of Kana of Galilee owed its name; it being famous for its strong reeds which provided ... the shafts for spears.

It seems likely, therefore, that the colloquial Hebrew idiom of the times referred to a spear as a reed. This opinion is strengthened by the fact that Arabic—a language closely related to Hebrew—uses the same word *'kana'* for a spear. Certainly a heavy, dripping sponge put on the point of a spear makes more sense than one on the drooping tip of a willowy hyssop.

The gospel of *John* is the only one which reports that Jesus' side was pierced by a spear and, as he claims to have been an eyewitness, great value must be placed on his testimony, although he is thought to have been mistaken.

As any lawyer with experience of accident, robbery and hold-up trials will confirm, the worst possible witness is another. Very seldom do two witnesses agree on what they have seen of an exciting or dramatic event; the more shocking the event the less reliable or corroborative the testimony, for each has 'seen' something different.

Assume that the author of *John*, present at the Crucifixion and shocked by the execution of Jesus, sees from a distant and possibly low-sited position, a soldier pointing up at Jesus a flashing spear or reed. Not knowing that he is passing-up a wine soaked sponge, he assumes that the soldier is about to plunge the weapon into the man on the Cross. When, a few seconds later, he sees bright red wine flowing down Jesus' naked body, he mistakes it for blood by sheer association of ideas. His trauma is complete and, forever after, he will swear that—as he sincerely believes—he saw that soldier thrust that spear into the Lord's side.

So, on the evidence of the gospels alone, there exists the strong possibility that a plan to cheat the Cross was operating at the Crucifixion. But how does one get a drugged, but still living, man off the Cross and smuggle him away under the watchful eyes, possibly, of hundreds? In the event the problem had an easy solution, remove the witnesses and you remove the problem. How does one banish witnesses from the place of public execution? This, too, is simple, change the place.

That this was actually done in the case of Jesus is no longer conjecture or speculation, but the hard-rock testimony of the gospels. The place *was* changed!

But, of course, before any of the foregoing happened, another essential part of the plan had to be set moving and in this, the chief character was no longer Jesus ... but Judas the Sicarii.

16 / Was Judas a Judas?

The most maligned man in the whole span of human history was Judas the Sicarii ... who was innocent!

It is altogether doubtful that any amount of evidence would ever convince the general mass of Christians that Judas—whether the Sicarii or Iscariot—did not betray Jesus, for to believe otherwise at this late stage would be to demolish the only myth that stands between the only explanation Christianity has discovered to explain Jesus' capture, and the historical truth.

And yet, the fact is that although the gospels make a big deal out of Judas' alleged betrayal—or appear to—they also severally describe a very strange scene during the Last Supper which makes it absolutely certain that he did not! It is this scene which has justified the opinion that the authorities in Jerusalem had agreed to exchange Jesus the son for Jesus the father, and that it had been Judas who had taken this message to Bethany.

Critical scholars have long been dubious about the justice of the accusation against Judas. Had Jesus been the Son of God, they argue, he must have possessed Divine Prescience and have known everything about the past, present and future. If that were so, they ask, how does one explain his calling as one of the Twelve the disciple who was later to betray him to a shameful death?

It is a very good question which, like many others similarly embarrassing to the faith, has been answered in the language of gobbledegook; this time it is explained that, being under the control of God—who had already decided what was to happen—Jesus wasn't accorded this insight into his fate. Which makes poor Judas the meat in the middle of the sandwich.

Acting, no doubt, on the principle that one can't have too much of a good thing, the gospel authors or their editors have documented Judas as a thorough, card-carrying rogue who, in addition to betraying the Lord, also had his fingers in the till. That this was calumny is best shown by the possibility that Judas had nothing to do with Jesus' funds for, with the disciple Levi-Matthew—who was Jesus' brother—a former tax gatherer used to handling vast sums of money and accounting for it, is it likely that the funds would have been handled by the Zealot assassin that Judas really was? Prescient the Lord might not have been, but he wasn't a fool!

Another reason for doubting the justice of the charge of betrayal against Judas—and this is both significant and eloquent—is the curious lack of any sign of anger or disgust in the other disciples at either him or his alleged act. All that is found is a mild and wondering curiosity towards the end of the gospel of *John* when Jesus is asked what will Judas do now that he is no longer with him, and Jesus smartly and tartly tells them to mind their own business. However, as this scene is with the *Risen* Jesus, its authenticity is to be doubted.

It is this total lack of human reaction on the disciples' part which arouses the suspicion that the true position might have been totally different from that pretended. It is strongly suggested that all Judas did was what he was *told* to do; that his role was merely that of a go-between negotiating Jesus' surrender in exchange for Jesus bar Abbas with the father's full knowledge and consent and, indeed, on his instructions.

What is certain about the matter is that Jesus had already decided to surrender to the authorities even *before* the Last Supper so that betrayal—as the word is understood—never really entered into the scheme of things.

Jesus had foregone the relative safety of Bethany to venture into a city teeming with spies, and to eat a meal at a house less than one hundred yards from that of the High Priest, who had already advocated to the Sanhedrin that it was expedient that Jesus should die. This being so, it was surely a little late in the day to be tossing around accusations of betrayal—in the future tense—when Jesus had already tossed the dice with Death.

The only plausible reason for him going anywhere near the danger area is that he had already decided to give himself up ... and the only plausible reason for *this* is that Jesus considered that he was getting a bargain.

Once launched on his journey to the Cross, all that remained to be done was to settle when and where his surrender would occur ... and by which of his disciples the news would be taken to the waiting authorities.

This part of Jesus' decision—if not all of it—must have met with violent protest for as their lather of anxiety shows in the gospel story, none was willing to earn the scorn of all Galilee by turning in his King and having the uninformed think that he had betrayed him.

But one of the Twelve had to do it—and did—so how was he selected?

Although the gospels differ on the method, there can be little argument against the suggestion that the problem was decided by a simple lottery; whether by Jesus handing a sop to the man he had chosen or, as two gospels relate, by selecting him who dipped into the bowl at the same time as he. However, as he is alleged to have told the disciples about the latter plan, it is against commonsense that this was done because all that—for example—Judas, were he the foul traitor of tradition, would needed to have done to avoid detection was *not* dip into the bowl when Jesus did. What would have become of the myth, then?

What probably happened was as *John* relates; that Jesus merely told them that one would have to do the unpleasant job and that he would nominate him by handing him the sop, an ancient form of 'eeny-meeny-miney-mo', perhaps.

Judas having been chosen, the other disciples evidently heaved sighs of relief for there is absolutely no hint of the violent reaction we would expect had a traitor been pointed out by Jesus, as the gospels pretend. All that happened was that Jesus said to the unfortunate Judas: 'Go quickly and do what thou *hast* to do!' In short, Judas had received his instructions *before* the betrayal scene. He knew what he had to do and, without another word, left for his date with destiny.

Soon after, Jesus and the remaining eleven left the house of the upper room and made their way to the Garden of Gethsemane ... where, carrying out his instructions, Judas later led the exultant Romans. How did Judas know they would be there? Why, if Judas were an odious informer, did Jesus not avoid arrest by simply keeping on walking, through Gethsemane and up over the Mount of Olives to the safety of Bethany? Instead, he hung around in the darkness of the garden actually *waiting* to be arrested. This is not the act to be expected of the victim of betrayal; it *is* that of one keeping his side of a bargain!

So no matter which way the alleged betrayal is looked at, it is explicable only on the grounds already stated, which are completely opposite to those claimed by the gospels.

Now arises the question of why, if Judas were guiltless, did he hang himself? Not only is it not at all certain that he did, but even a century ago a prominent New Testament commentator wrote: 'In the absence of evidence, a horrible end for Judas would inevitably have been invented! We say that it *was* ... and that the gospel authors merely repeated it. However, there's little doubt that his brother Zealots—not knowing the real story—would have taken a swift revenge. The Sicarii—so-called because they were assassins armed with wickedly sharp, curved daggers called '*sicar*'—undoubtedly struck him down one dark night, or even in the broad light of day, soon after. In fact, the tradition repeated in the gospels that: 'all his bowels fell out' strongly suggests that his belly was ripped open, by the favourite plunging upward stroke of the Sicarii.

A great deal has always been made out of Jesus' Agony in the Garden of Gethsemane as he awaited the coming of his betrayer and the enemy. As we have already seen that Jesus would not have been there had he not wished, and could have escaped several times over during the hours of waiting—during which his disciples slept—what was the nature of this 'agony' likely to have been? Eliminating all possibility of any supernatural telepathy between Jesus and God, why was Jesus sweating on this cool night of a Judean spring? The gospels report variously on the events that occurred in the garden that night, but only *Luke* describes this sweating in dramatic and exaggerated terms: '. . . and his sweat was as it were great drops of blood falling down to the ground.'

This obvious hyperbole was used to provide a graphic comparison of the intensity and volume of Jesus' sweat which fell like great clots of blood from an open wound; it was never intended that the phrase should be taken literally, as the carefully selected words show. This, however, has not prevented the faith from asserting that Jesus had actually sweated blood which, as far as medical science is concerned—the legends of the Stigmata notwithstanding—is impossible. Such cases as have been claimed to have occurred with, for example, hystero-epileptics, have not been authenticated. To claim that Jesus was such would be to go against every grain of evidence to the contrary in all four gospels.

There's no doubt that Jesus had excellent cause to sweat, but it must have been with fear, not only of that shadow of the Cross looming over him, but that either the Romans might not come—suspecting a Zealot trap—or that they would arrive so late that this timetable would be disrupted If the delay were of a serious nature, the whole plan to cheat the Cross would be ruined, for Governor Pontius Pilatus might postpone the execution until Sunday. Should this occur, Jesus would inevitably be nailed to the Cross to hang in agony for days, then, to die.

It must have been with great relief that he, at last, saw the bobbing lanterns dancing in the darkness as their bearers emerged from the wall and come ever closer along the Kidron Valley towards the Garden where he waited.

That it must have been, by then, about 3 a.m. our time on the orthodox Thursday (so *John*) rather than the same time a day later—as declared by the Synoptic gospels— seems evident from the impossible timetable of these books.

According to these three testimonies, Jesus went to the Cross at our 9 a.m., so that only six hours were left for him to be marched back to the far side of the City to the house of Caiaphas—where Peter did *not* hear the cock crow for the keeping of fowls was illegal in Jerusalem— and for the other events to take place. He had to be examined and grilled by Caiaphas, undergo his impossible trial before the Sanhedrin—which wasn't permitted to assemble during the hours of darkness—be taken before Pilate, then to Antipas and back to Pilate, sentenced, handed over to the troops for scourging and to be dressed up as a mock-king, then to make his painful way to Golgotha dragging his Cross and, at last after all that, to be Crucified. Six hours, for all *that?*

Quite apart from the sheer incredibility of some of the events—and getting even either, let alone both, Pilate or Antipas out of bed before dawn is one of them—the whole timetable of events is so compressed that it must be regarded as no more than a *precis* of what occurred between his arrest and his execution. The suggestion that they all occurred in a mere six hours is not to be taken seriously.

Intent on deleting all references to the Essenic Paschal Feast, which Jesus actually ate on Wednesday night, the gospel authors—or their editors—had to make the Last Supper appear to have been the Orthodox Paschal Feast eaten on Friday night (the beginning of the Jewish Saturday, Sabbath and, in this case, the Passover). This, in turn, required that Jesus be sent to the Cross the very next morning ... with the result that he stood crucified on an utterly impossible day!

The timetable in *John* allows a full day for the trials instead of the Synoptics' frugal and incredible six hours and, in addition, states that Jesus went to the Cross at about noon on Friday—three hours later or twenty-one hours earlier—than the time set by the agreeable trio. If, then, a full day were used up in Jesus' examination by the Sanhedrin—this time, in legal daylight—followed by his curious quizzing by Pilate and Herod Antipas, with Jesus plainly wasting time by bamboozling them with his doubletalk, this left Friday morning for Pilate to sum up and give his verdict which, being a much more reasonable chronology, is that much more likely to be correct.

Nor is it altogether wise to dismiss the possibility that Pontius Pilate was a conniving party to the protracted proceedings; there is still the reverence in which he was held by the early Church to be explained, as well as the very strong tradition that, not only were he and his wife more 'secret' disciples of Jesus, but that Pilate was 'got at' with a sizeable bribe, rumoured to have been $60,000. In view of what, we say, actually happened—and much more significant evidence still remains to be presented—Pilate seems to have had a vested interest of *some* kind in the drama taking place in Jerusalem that day; certainly he wasn't looking after the interests of Tiberius Caesar ... and some of the Jews had to jolt his elbow to remind him where his real duty lay.

It will probably come as a severe shock to most Christians to discover that Pontius Pilate—the man who is supposed to have sent Jesus to the Cross with a quick rinse of the hands—was so highly thought of by the early Christian Church that, even today, the Coptic Church of both Egypt and Ethiopia holds 25 June of each year as Holy to his name and memory. Perhaps the same is true of the

Greek Orthodox Church. Pilate's wife, said to have been Claudia Procla, is similarly honoured. Why?

After stalling around, going from Jesus in the Judgment Hall outside to the Sanhedrin members who—significantly—wouldn't enter that place and so defile their pre-Passover purity, back and forth, and forth and back, scuttled Judea's Governor like some urchin errand boy until, unable to stall any longer, the amiable Pilate faced up to the inevitable and, at last, delivered the only penalty he could ... death!

As Rome stood guard over the civil laws of Judea and the right to impose the death penalty, only the religious Law was left to the Sanhedrin to administer. As Jesus was sentenced to death, it follows that his crime must have offended the civil law of Rome rather than—as the gospels pretend—the religious law. As he certainly wasn't charged with murder, the only other civil crime left in the book worthy of the death sentence was insurrection and treason against Rome by endeavouring to restore the Hasmonean Throne. The penalty for this was exactly that imposed.

'And Pilate wrote a title, and put it on the Cross. And the writing was: JESUS OF NAZARETH THE KING OF THE JEWS ... and it was written in Hebrew, and Greek and Latin. Then said the chief priests of the Jews to Pilate: "Write not KING OF THE JEWS, but that he *said* I am King of the Jews!" '

The wily Pilate, brushing off their pleas, said: 'What I have writ, I have writ!'

It seems that Pilate must have known more about the Hasmoneans and their importance in Judean history than the gospels give him credit for.

By the time the verdict was handed down, Jesus bar Abbas was probably at liberty under his father's deal with Pilate and might even have been at Bethany trying to console his mother, who was determined to witness her husband's execution. With Mary the Mother of Jesus and her sister Salome, Mary of Bethany slowly set off for Golgotha.

And as they descended the Mount of Olives, there through the Golden Gate and into the Kidron, came a small group of soldiers ... and a man carrying on his bleeding shoulders the *patibulem* or horizontal cross piece of the instrument of his execution. The two groups merged and slowly proceeded ... where?

17 / Death in the Garden

'And he bearing his cross went forth into a place called
The Place of a Skull, which is called in the Hebrew, *Golgotha*.'

Wrong!

All four gospels state that Jesus was crucified at Golgotha, which they 'interpret from the Hebrew' as meaning
'the place of a skull' or some similar variant, and imply
that this was the place of public execution; while it should
have been, it was not!

As a result of this error—or misrepresentation—most
Christians have envisaged it as a bare and tortured rock,
littered with the bones of its dead, and shunned by man,
beast and even the birds. Recollect any artist's graphic
Crucifixion painting and Golgotha always is portrayed as a
'skull' of rock, starkly etched with its burden of three
crosses, silhouetted against a sullen sky.

Now, for the real picture of Golgotha, described by one
who was there on that day, read *John* 19:40.

'Now in the place where he was crucified there was a
garden, and in the *garden* a new sepulchre wherein was
never man yet laid.'

The public killing ground in a *garden*? That Golgotha
was not the place of public execution can quickly be
shown, as can the fact that this name had nothing whatever to do with 'skull' which, in Hebrew, is *'Gulgoleth'*.

As the sepulchre or tomb belonged to Joseph of Arimathea so must the garden in which it stood, and it is this
one fact which alone makes it absolutely certain that this
was *not* the site of public executions ... which were always held in some *public* place. To hold a contrary opinion is to make nonsense of reason. Moreover, nobody
aware of the Jew's religious abhorrence of dead bodies
would, for even one second, consider the proposition that
Joseph's tomb stood in or even near the public launching

119

pad for all those bound for eternity. Such a place would be anathema to a Jew, who would have been just as likely to curse God as to build his own future tomb amid the bones of the wretches whose fate had been crucifixion and were therefore accursed in the sight of God.

Yet this was the place in which Pilate had decreed that Jesus was to die: in a private garden which, at the proper time, its owner could order the public to quit ... and perhaps they were not even admitted but were forced to watch proceedings from some distance off. That this private garden was owned by the very same man who was a secret disciple of Jesus and who would later ask Pilate for permission to take down the body of Jesus, does nothing to diminish the deep suspicion that something very unusual was going on.

And when, eventually, Joseph made his request for Jesus' body, he referred to it by the Greek word 'soma,' which means a living body, while—probably for the benefit of the waiting and listening Roman centurion—Pilate is particular to use the Greek word 'ptoma', which means 'a corpse.' A small detail in itself, perhaps, but it looms large when placed alongside the rest of the curiously suspicious evidence.

Joseph of Arimathea was a man of means and he obviously had hold of Pilate's ear. While it is too much to suggest that he was the man behind the bribe story, he might have been; at all events, his relationship with the Roman Governor was apparently such that it would have been a comparatively simple matter for him to have suggested that a change of venue might be politically wise for the execution of the popular aspirant for the Hasmonean Throne. If carried out at the usual spot, his crucifixion might well have started another riot and, with all those Zealots in town, who could tell what might happen?

That Pilate's agreement must have been won—no matter by what means—is indicated by the place that was chosen; that two other Zealots were crucified at the same time could have been merely a device to put the imprimatur of a public execution on what, clearly, was a very private one. In addition to Tiberius Caesar having a long arm, his 'ear' was extremely sensitive to sounds from afar.

This speculation must be very close to the truth for it is surely stretching too far the fibres of coincidence to suggest that, in deciding to substitute a private for the public place of execution, Pilate should have 'happened' to select the garden owned by the only member of the Sanhedrin definitely known to have been Jesus' secret disciple. As the owner of the place, Joseph's permission must have been sought, if not offered. Thus he and Pilate at least had a meeting of some kind before the decision was made.

In the days of Jesus, the word 'garden' (Heb. *'gen'*) had a very precise meaning and conditions had to meet the definitive requirements before the noun was applied; not just any old lot strewn with weeds—or even filled with flowers—qualified. Before a place could properly be called a 'garden' two essential requirements had to be met: it must be surrounded by a wall of some kind, and some form of irrigation—natural or artificial—must flow through the compound. The Garden of Gethsemane might have been the perfect example if we can assume that it had a wall, for it almost certainly sat astride the brook Kidron *in those days.*

The presently shown Gethsemane is too far up the first slopes of the Mount of Olives ever to have qualified and, besides, it is only one of the *two* 'authentic' Gardens of Gethsemane which existed a century ago. Crazy though it seems, in those days the two great rivals within orthodox Christianity—the Church in Rome and the Greek Orthodox—each maintained its own separate 'true' site and one can easily imagine the great grandfathers of the present huckster-guides flagging down the tourists with shrill protests of: 'May God strike me dead if I tell you a lie, sah . . .' It is unlikely, whatever God did about the matter, that either could have been authentic.

Suppose that we now take a rather close look at this rather odd name *'Gethsemane'*. Reference books will tell you that this compound Hebrew word means 'the olive oil press', on the score that *'gth'*, *'gath'* or *'geth'* means 'press'—which it does—and that *'semane'* means 'olive oil', which it does not! The latter is correctly rendered *'shemen zayith'* while the fruit or berry which produces it is called *'zeth shemen'* or 'the oil olive'. While this might seem to be close enough in sound to *'gethsemane'* to make any further pursuit of the matter unnecessary, there is a tremendous trifle contained in the difference between the two words *'shemen'* and *'semane';* the first-named always referring to oil extracted from the olive. Shortly, we shall discover what *'semane'* meant.

Olives were first trampled or bruised in a mortar to extract the finest first flood of oil, then packed into woven containers which were put into a pit and subjected to great pressure by means of a long lever weighted with a heavy stone. In such a way was the last drop of oil extracted. These, of course, were the green olives; the black is not a separate variety but is merely the over-ripe green and is practically useless for oil production.

Now there was another kind of oil extensively used in Judea—the aromatic oil of fragrant plants, shrubs and flowers—which was extracted by totally different methods. The raw material was squashed to a pulp by a heavy, wheellike stone disc or 'gol' running backwards and forwards in a stone channel or trough. When the mess was thoroughly pulverised boiling water was added and the oil floated on top. This was then skimmed off and run into large earthenware jars or vats.

One of the fragrantissimas so treated was the sweet-smelling White Jasmine which Hebrew calls either by exactly the same name, or 'jessamine'. It requires no great amount of study to see that the latter word, broken down into the syllables 'jes-same-in-e', comes very close indeed to 'geth-sem-an-e' which, after all, has been filtered through at least one other language before arriving at our spelling and pronunciation. For reasons soon to be explained, the difference in vowels is of no significance. It is interesting to notice that in Arabic—whose relationship to Hebrew has already been mentioned—'Gethsemane' is called 'el Jes-man-i-yeh' which seems to be conclusive evidence that what we call the 'Garden of Gethsemane' was once known simply as the 'Jasmine Garden', because it was devoted to the growing of the 'jasminum officinale' or White Jasmine and to the extraction of its fragrant oil.

All of which might, to some, seem to be a great to-do about nothing very important when, in fact, the contrary is the case for it is in the method of extracting the oil of jasmine that we discover the Garden's more commonly used name, which turns out to be quite astonishing.

We have already noted that the name of the wheel-like stone disc which rolled back and forth crushing the plants was 'gol.' This noun derives from the extensively used Hebrew root 'gl' which was applied to anything of a circular nature, of which 'galgal' (wheel) and the roughly circular shape of both the lake and the province of Galilee are typical examples.

At once the wheel-like stone *'gol'* reminds us of another wheel-like stone disc mentioned by *Matthew* 28:60 '. . . and then he (Joseph of Arimathea) rolled a great stone to the door of the sepulchre and departed.'

Several examples of these 'great stones' have been found, some still standing in the groove in which they were rolled, to and fro, to open or close the doorway into the sepulchre or tomb.

Here we must amplify our earlier remark about the significance of the Hebrew vowel. Written Hebrew had no real vowels until about one thousand years ago; up until then they made certain consonants do double duty. As an example of the sort of trouble a vowel-less written language could lead to, imagine that English had the same impediment and that one wanted to write, for example, 'red', which could be 'rd'. However, anyone reading what had been written would have only the sense of what both pre and pro-ceeded the word 'rd' to tell whether it meant *red, rid, rod, arid, rude, rode, road, raid, reed, read, erode* or even *rodeo*' . . . and, possibly, there are others.

Keeping this well in mind, we take another look at the mystery name 'Golgotha', which the gospels claim meant 'skull' or 'place of the skull'. As was pointed out, this meaning is impossible because 'skull' was *'gulgoleth!'* So what did the word mean?

Without vowels, 'Golgotha' was spelled *'Glgth'* which just happens to be the way in which two Hebrew words *'Gol'* meaning the wheel-like stone disc used in the Jasmine Garden, and *'geth'* meaning a press, would be spelled when linked together—*'Glgth.'* So, to us, at least, it seems that the colloquial name for the Jasmine Garden was *'Golgeth'*—the wheelpress—and not *'Golgotha'*, the place of the skull.

Now the impossibility of Joseph of Arimathea building his own tomb in the garden, vanishes because we have, it is submitted, proved a reasonable case that it would have stood close by his fragrant wheelpress and *not* in the place of public execution.

If we are correct in naming and identifying the true location of Golgeth, it means that Jesus was executed privately somewhere in the Valley of the Kidron, and probably hard by the 'pinnacle' of the Temple from which, some thirty years later, his brother James-Jacob was cast and stoned to death and, according to written tradition, buried at this very spot.

Strange to relate, among several ancient Jewish tombs still standing nearby today, is that reputed to belong to St. James, the Lord's brother. As this will be discussed in some detail later, all that need be remarked here is that there exists a very strong possibility that this, in a less elaborate form than we see it today, was originally Joseph of Arimathea's 'new tomb in which never yet was man laid' and which served for the 'burial' of Jesus.

Nor are we alone in our thinking on the whole general subject, although ours has been arrived at by a totally new route. The noted scholar, archaeologist and scroll expert, John Allegro, also inclines towards the Gethsemane location for the Crucifixion. In his book, *The Dead Sea Scrolls*, he tells of a certain Zadok, who might have been the founder of the Essenes who, among other appellations, called themselves 'Sons of Zadok'. Interestingly enough, Jesus numbered a Zadok among his ancestors though whether or not he was the same man whom the Essenes revered as the persecuted—and possibly martyred— 'Teacher of Righteousness' it is impossible to say.

John Allegro reports the finding in the Dead Sea region several years ago of a unique copper scroll on whose soft metal surface had been inscribed a mass of valuable information, including directions for locating what could well be the lost treasure of the Jerusalem Temple reputed to have been hidden by the priests shortly before the destruction of the City by the Romans in September of A.D. 70.

Apparently this scroll lists more than *sixty* separate hoards of gold and of silver amounting in all to some two hundred *tons* and probably worth today—if it is still to be found—somewhere in the vicinity of $160,000,000. What is of even greater interest of immediate moment is this scroll's revelation that in precisely the same area as where St. James' reputed tomb stands was what is called 'The Garden of Zadok' and that in his garden was . . . his tomb!

So here we have a possible ancestor of Jesus who was the founder—and perhaps the martyred leader—of the Essenes from whose midst emerged his cousin, John the Baptist, having both his garden and his tomb on or near the very spot where both the 'Jasmine Garden' and 'Golgeth' were; where Jesus was crucified and where was also the tomb in which he was 'buried'. Add to this the possibility that his brother, James-Jacob was buried in the very same tomb and you have a mass of circumstances too coincidental to be casual. On this, hear John Allegro, in his book *The Dead Sea Scrolls* (Pelican 1964).

'If the Garden of the Agony was attached, like Zadok's, to the tomb of a rich Jew, we should perhaps link Gethsemane with Golgotha and the sepulchre of Joseph of Arimathea closer geographically than the traditional, documentarily-unfounded locations at present allow.'

Less cautious than he, we say that they are identical!

18 / Joseph the Mystery-man

Deeds speaking louder than words, what a man does often defines what he is and, sometimes, even who he is!

Although the gospels are surprisingly reticent about Joseph of Arimathea considering the vital role he played after the Crucifixion—and must have played even before—it was by what he did in the final hour immediately before sunset on that first 'Good Friday' that we are able to track down our man ... with astonishing results!

We are told that this Joseph was both a rich man and a member of the powerful Jewish Sanhedrin or government—which makes him a 'somebody'—yet, at the very same time, that he was also one of Jesus' secret disciples. Even this meagre amount of information contains some shocks and generates two questions which, as far as is known, have never been satisfactorily answered, by the Church or anyone else.

How was it possible for this man to have been any kind of a disciple of Jesus, who made such a strong point of the utter inability of the wealthy to enter the 'Kingdom of God'?

Again, if Jesus' 'mission' were as innocent as it is claimed to have been, why was it necessary for Joseph to have kept his espousal of him and his cause a secret?

Another question demanding an answer is why this wealthy, important man who clearly had been acting as a spy for up to three years—depending on the duration of Jesus' 'mission'—and was thus betraying the Jewish Government, should suddenly blow his cover and thereby imperil both his fortune and his life when Jesus, apparently and officially, was dead and Joseph could be of no further use to him? Was it respect for his dead leader? Or was it compassion for his still-living King?

Right up until the hour before sunset he had gone to elaborate pains to conceal his association with Jesus yet the moment he could no longer serve a living man, he incredibly revealed himself by this apparently useless act which was not only in breach of the Law of Judaism, but would earn the Sanhedrin's swift and savage retribution. And all for what? Merely to give decent burial to a man who should have had no further interest in whether he was buried or not?

Mark well that it was Joseph and his companion, Nicodemus—yet another secret disciple and probable Sanhedrin member—who actually and astonishingly removed Jesus' 'body' from the Cross, instead of the official Roman executioner, whose job this was. They did not merely receive the 'body' after he had taken it down; it was they who literally took it down! Why?

Was it so that the executioner wouldn't detect that Jesus was still breathing?

Note too, that it was the same pair who brushed aside the bystanding group of women of Jesus' family—whose traditional duty it was to prepare the body for burial—and themselves attended to this women's work. Was it for the selfsame reason?

The fact that by even touching the body they were deliberately defiling and making themselves ceremoniously unclean an hour before the Passover began, thus making their participation in the Holy Paschal Feast impossible, doesn't seem to have worried them any more than had the other perils to which they were exposing themselves.

Joseph of Arimathea's most daring act, however—unless it was all pre-arranged—was to go to the awesome Roman Governor and ask for the body. Their conversation was conducted in Greek and in our records of the event—also written in Greek—Josephus had the effrontery to ask for Jesus' *living* body *(soma)*. Swiftly Pilate corrected him and referred to it as a dead body *(ptoma)*. However, it is obvious that he knew it all to be a charade—or suspected something like that—for he turned to the centurion who had just come from the Cross with Joseph and, after expressing astonishment that Jesus could have died so quickly, asked the centurion was he really dead? Reassured by a centurion who obviously knew how many denarii made five hundred, Pilate gave his assent to Joseph . . . and the grand plan marched on!

Our suspicion as to what was going on is strengthened by the fact that the Law of Judaism commanded that none but a certain classification of person—apart from women, who didn't count—should come at a *dead* body. Furthermore, this Law held that whoever had been crucified had suffered a shameful death and was ever more accursed by God ... as was Jesus, the alleged Son of God. Thus, any Jew touching his body would have been similarly accursed. Because of this, it can confidently be asserted that Jesus was not dead.

The Jews had such a horror of such things that a victim's heartbroken family could stolidly watch as the executioner removed his corpse and tossed it into the waggon to be carted off to Gehenna, there to be fought over by the flames and the snarling mongrels of Jerusalem. Not a hand was ever lifted by the loving to give a crucified man a decent burial ... which makes Joseph of Arimathea's action even more astonishing ... but for one possibility.

Had Joseph made his request to Pilate in the way reported in the gospels, shrewd old Pontius—wise by now in the ways and customs of the Jews—would immediately have said: 'Why? What's this man to you?' What would have been the reply?

The sole exception which the Judaistic Law made to the rule that no male Jew should come at a dead body—most of all, at a crucified dead body—was that *this was permitted to the victim's closest-available eldest male relative.*

Is this the explanation? When Joseph and Nicodemus touched the body of Jesus either they broke the Law or they did not. If they did not, then it must have been because either Jesus was not dead or, if he were, they were closely related to him and qualified to be excepted. Conversely, if they were not related and excepted, there can be only one reason why they did not break the Law and that is that Jesus was not dead!

Of course, there's no reason in the world why they could not have been related *and* Jesus still alive!

If they were related to him, what was this relationship likely to have been? All that can be said with any certainty is that it must necessarily have been a close one. Nicodemus can now never be traced for, in the absence of other clues, his assumed Greek name effectively buries him for all time, but what of Joseph of Arimathea? Well, we certainly now know him a great deal better than the gospels appear to—or admit—and there's still more information to come.

Consider this man. Rich, powerful and well connected with ready access to the ear of the Roman Governor of all Judea and, almost certainly, the owner of a very prosperous essential oil extraction garden called 'Golgeth', which suggests that he was of the Hasmoneans. This thought is reinforced by *Luke* 23:51 which ends, speaking of Joseph: '. . . who also himself waited for the Kingdom of God.', which takes it beyond reasonable doubt that he was, indeed, one of the Hasmonean clan. The *Luke* reference can only mean that he, too, was a Messianist, which is a pretty apt and concise description of the Hasmoneans for it said much in little.

The suggestion that a Hasmonean was 'in trade' would be no more than a restatement of the historical facts. We have it on the authority of Josephus—himself a Hasmonean—that when Herod the Great stole their throne about seventy years before, he also 'inherited' a vast amount of their real estate including a most prosperous balsam garden in the Jericho area. From this it would seem that the Hasmoneans pretty well had the oil extraction business sewn up. The enmity which existed between Josephus and a man called John of Gischala—another Hasmonean —was due to the historian's jealousy that the crafty John had cornered the olive oil business for the whole of Galilee, if not all Judea, and was raking it in. Just what Herod's windfall might have been worth is indicated by what happened when Marc Antony took it away from him to placate the greedy and lascivious Cleopatra. Herod had no qualms about leasing it back from her at an annual rental of $200,000 . . . which suggests that it must have been quite an operation. And this, remember, was *two thousand* years ago!

Perhaps the one piece of Hasmonean real estate which not even Herod dared seize because of the sacred family tombs it contained was the 'King's Garden' in the Kidron Valley, which we identify with both the 'Garden of Zadok' and the 'Jasmine Garden'. What is more likely than that the Hasmonean survivors later found the oil business the only way to make a living after their throne and other assets were stolen. Their ownership of a large part of the Kidron Valley might have provided the perfect location being, as it was, right alongside the Temple.

The probability that Joseph of Arimathea was a close relative of Jesus is enhanced by another strange feature of his alleged behaviour: his readiness to place a dead Jesus in his own tomb. This was an action totally alien to the Jewish ethos. In those days it was unthinkable and abhorrent that any Jew would willingly permit himself to be buried in other than the family tomb. When the time came for him to die, no matter how distant from his home he might be, the Jew would head for the family village and crawl into the ancestral tomb.

Even more interestingly, the Jew of those times had an even greater abhorrence of burying a *stranger* in *his* tomb. As 'stranger' meant someone not of his own family, would Joseph have given Jesus a place in his own tomb had they *not* been closely related? This is so unlikely as to practically guarantee that they were of the same blood.

Not a little of the mystery that has surrounded this Joseph of Arimathea would seem to have been created by scholars who have sought in his name a clue to where he came from. There has been an enormous amount of argument over this but the matter has been resolved by settling for the town of Rentis, in the hill country of Samaria. This has been justified by taking as a clue the first part of his name, *Arima* and claiming that it derived from *'Rama'*, *'Rumah'* or *'Ramah,'* all of which names meant 'a high place'. Although true that these have the meaning of mountainous or hill country, they much more frequently mean 'places of religious worship'. This genteel phrase conceals the old pagan practice of erecting a giant phallus in order to worship the god or gods of fertility. As more 'respectable' influences developed, the phallus shrank to a mere heap of stones or a short pillar and, eventually, became the familiar altar.

These 'high places' referred to the nature or style of the object of worship rather than to its locale, and they were probably originally erected on flat country as often as they were on hilly. However, there is an even more fatal flaw in the identification of Rentis as Joseph's town.

Despite Jesus' charitable attitude towards Samaritans, these people were held in contempt and abhorrence by the Hebrews; if Joseph had belonged to their 'race' he most certainly would not have been a member of the Sanhedrin, sitting in government and in judgment over God's anointed Jews. If it be claimed that Joseph was a 'secret' Samaritan, as he had been a secret disciple of Jesus, it is demolished by the simple fact that if scholars almost two thousand years later have been able to identify him as a Samaritan by his name, his contemporaries would have found it even easier. So that it seems that we shall have to look elsewhere for Joseph's home town.

Suppose that, instead of seeking a clue *within* his name, we take the entire name and look for a town or village of the same or a similar name which might have existed in 1st century Judea. As Joseph, we say, was a close relative of Jesus, we look first to Galilee and speculatively eye the Plain of Gennesareth where, we again say, was once the village of Jesus' birthplace—'*en Nasira*'—which was soon engulfed by bustling, expanding Capernaum. As families in those days tended to congregate in the same area, we wonder was there ever a town or village on the Plain of Gennesareth which might be identified with Arimathea.

And there was!

A few tumbled stones lying in the grass near to the authentic site of Capernaum is all that remains of the ancient village of '*Areimeh*' which, it is suggested, seems a much more plausible place for an Arimathean to come from than Rentis, in odious Samaria.

Having traced Joseph with reasonable centainty to Areimeh, we now have to face up to his actual relationship to Jesus. Considering what has so far been demonstrated about this 'strange' man, it is thought that it might not be unreasonable to see him as an uncle of Jesus on his father's side, and so the brother of Alpheus-Jacob. As we know of only one man who was brother to Jesus' father, there is little we can do but identify Joseph of Arimathea with the very same Joseph who was once the betrothed husband of Mary, whom he divorced by secret '*git*' when he found her with child to another man, his own brother Alpheus.

Although not yet done with Joseph of Arimathea we now move on to that strange, unique group of ancient tombs which still stand in the Kidron Valley between the eastern wall of the Holy City and the Mount of Olives. Passing by that said to belong to Zechariah, father of Jesus' cousin John the Baptist, we arrive at the reputed tomb of Jesus' brother, James-Jacob, and gaze up at it, speculatively.

Why does this small group of interrelated tombs stand here? Why are these so opulent compared with the thousands of others surrounding them, which are so mean? If

there were others equally imposing at one time, why have
they vanished and only these—said to have been those of
members of the one 'family'—suffered to remain? Was it
because the 'family' was that of the Hasmonean Kings?

The reputed tomb of St. James stands as a Graeco-Roman styled pinnacled edifice which has literally been carved
out of the rock shelf which surrounds it on three sides.
Set low in its facade is what might once have been its
original entrance in front of which, on a distant day, a
discarded stone presswheel might have rolled; this way on
Friday, that way on Sunday.

The claim that this was, in fact, the tomb of St. James
is disputed by some scholars who say that, to the contrary,
it belonged to the *'bene Hezir'* or 'Sons of Hezir', a priestly family whose lineage goes back to at least 480 B.C.
when many of those deported to Babylon returned to
Jerusalem.

Now there's no doubt at all that *'Hezir'* was all that has
been claimed; it was, in fact, seventeenth in the order of
importance and thus was the third last of the only twenty
families who could prove their genealogies on the return
from deportation.

However, to assert that this was their tomb is to claim
the impossible for the building dates from only the 1st
century A.D. . . . which was when Joseph built *his* tomb in
this general area. Ascribing the tomb to the 'Sons of
Hezir' might be due to a complete misunderstanding of
what *'bene Hezir'* really signified, for the expression can
also be translated to mean 'Sons of the Crown', which
opens up interesting possibilities.

Sons of what Crown?

The Hebrew *'hezir'* was the slim golden circlet worn on
the head of both an Israelite King into battle, and the
same emblem worn on the brow of the High Priest.

Only the Hasmoneans combined both offices!

Seeing both Jesus and his brother James-Jacob—who
certainly was High Priest before his death—as prominent
members of the Hasmonean family, as we do, and both
'Sons of the Crown' the argument that the tomb belonged
to the *'bene Hezir'* is more favourable to identification of
this as St. James' sepulchre than it is against it. Being
James', it was—temporarily—Jesus' before him and, originally, the very one built for himself by Joseph of Arimathea.

And why did Joseph build his tomb here at Jerusalem instead of back in Galilee at Ariemeh, near to Capernaum?

Having been driven from the village and the area by ridicule arising from his enforced divorce and the obvious condition of Mary—and a cuckolded husband is still worth a snigger in any community two thousand years later—Joseph must have shaken the dust of Gennesareth off his feet. Putting down new roots in Jerusalem, he began a new life which was to lead to prosperity and civic importance. And so the many years passed until he met the son of his brother ... the son of Mary whom once he had loved. Isn't it natural that a devout Jew should have felt the pull of kin and of warm blood more than the icy chill of jealousy?

Being a Hasmonean he would naturally support him whom they recognised as their King, irrespective of his personal relationship to him.

Although Joseph of Arimathea's part in the conspiracy can only be guessed at, it evidently fooled not only the Jewish Sanhedrin and the Romans, but has continued to fool the Christian world ever since.

19 / Escape from the Tomb

It can hardly be claimed by the most enthusiastic of evangelists that Christianity has been a smashing success and has set men's minds afire!

Entirely putting aside the many foul deeds done in the name of Holy Jesus and his Glory by generations of monstrous men of God with their dripping swords and ghastly, flaring matchsticks, the brutal facts of life over which the Church must ponder are these: that after one thousand nine hundred years of 'hard-sell' the promise of Eternal Life has still not been 'bought' by any more than about twenty-five per cent of the present world population; that if hard answers were demanded of the approximately 800,-000,000 who profess to be Christians, it would be found that only about half of them are sincere and devout believers who daily practice Christ's alleged precepts.

The others are what might be called 'Census-Christians' who so describe themselves for a variety of strange reasons including 'because one has to say *something!*' and 'Christianity is respectable,' and 'it is so socially right!' Still others, pressed to explain their lack of faith would vaguely answer: 'Oh, *I* don't know . . !' But they *do* know, for the root of their reason is that they *can* not and *do* not and *will* not believe that Jesus rose from the dead.

As the English theologian J. S. Bezzant has put it: 'The secular outlook of uneducated and unreflective people often makes them feel, when they hear talk of life after death, that they are being put off their rights in this world by cheques drawn on the Bank of Heaven, the solvency of which they greatly doubt.'

While Mr. Bezzant has hit the nail smack on the head, it is odd that a theologian should complain at the inability of the ignorant masses to comprehend the abstract concepts which theology itself has devised for, as he has also written: 'Divine revelation . . . implies the human reception and understanding of it for what it is. It is a fatal objection that there can be Divine revelation which is unassimilable by human understanding. Alleged revelation which is incomprehensible, whatever else it may be, is not *revelation.*' The same, presumably, should also apply to human revelation.

It seems altogether strange that Jesus apparently had no trouble making himself understood by simple, ignorant Galileans yet theology, which seeks to explain Jesus who should not be in need of it, finds itself unable to communicate with all but a 'few' Christians whom, we suspect, don't know very much about it, either. If people don't believe, it might not be due so much to their inability to follow Jesus, as to follow the theologians.

The known history of Jesus surely ended with the empty tomb; all the rest, however Divinely revealed or inspired, is theological speculation expressed in terms of the supernatural otherworld. Finding the stone rolled aside and the tomb empty, theology very promptly moved in and has lived rent free ever since. From the world's very best address—#1 Jerusalem—has come a flood of esoteric abstract concepts over the centuries, pretending to explain the inexplicable, but merely turning Jesus' demand of a new way of life for the *living,* into a grab bag of vague promises for the dead.

Any suspicious cheques that have been drawn on the Bank of Heaven, if not forged in God's name, have been counter-signed by theology.

After nineteen centuries of their philosophical guessing games the theologians have mucked-up everything to such an extent that what started out as a simple act of restoration has become a gigantic tangle of plain lies and confused truths, and a simple man of his times has been turned not only into God, but also into the greatest bore the world has known.

Tell people that Jesus rose from the dead and, later, ascended physically up to heaven before the astonished eyes of his disciples, and you don't tell them of two wonders which actually happened; you tell them that this is what theology *says* happened. Both the Resurrection and the Ascension are statements of theology and not those of history. As such, they are no more likely to be right than wrong. They are no more likely to be right on this—perhaps less so—than they were about the earth being flat and the centre of the universe. Once they catch on to the fact that a body needs to attain a velocity of 25,000 m.p.h. to escape from the earth's gravitational pull and they'll have the Ascension licked, too!

Perhaps those who disbelieve the Resurrection are right to do so because—as has been shown—there are many more reasons to doubt that it happened than exist for believing that it did and, moreover, this was so right from the very beginning.

Finding the tomb empty at dawn that Sunday, Mary called Magdalene's first and natural reaction was to think that the sepulchre had been robbed and Jesus' body stolen. Shocked, she ran and brought Peter and another disciple to see the empty tomb. As *John* 20:1-10 explains the scene, the two men were of the same opinion as Mary: 'For as yet they knew not the Scripture that he must rise again from the dead. Then the disciples went away again unto their own home.' And that was that!

What *John* means is that the effect of the empty tomb—irrespective of the cause—was explicable only in the terms of prophecy no matter what had actually happened.

Though the other gospels have Mary and certain others find the tomb not empty, but with at least one 'angel' inside—though Jesus' body was gone—it is quite plain from *John* that there was no thought in their minds of resurrection in either of the forms envisaged by Judaism. Even when Mary later met the 'risen' Jesus she mistook him for the gardener, so that it is abundantly clear from all this that she and at least two disciples explained the empty tomb in natural terms; the body was gone, therefore it had been stolen.

However, Mary could not have thought this for very long, for the moment she recognised Jesus it must have been obvious to her that there had been no body to steal; that the very fact that Jesus was standing talking to her—a living, breathing man—meant that he had never been dead!

Now let us be very precise about this. Mary was a Jew and her mental reactions and thoughts must have been conditioned absolutely by what she, as a Jew, both knew and believed. As has already been explained but can't too often be emphasised, the Jews had a very precise definition of resurrection—both general or collective, and individual—and while death was most certainly the prerequisite condition for all involved in general resurrection, except those living at the moment it occurred, it was the avoidance or escape from death which defined an act of individual resurrection.

From the evidence of the gospels, Jesus met that condition perfectly.

As the Christian concept of Resurrection as applied to Jesus was foreign to Judaism and entirely the brainchild of St. Paul, it is quite impossible that Mary or the disciples could have conceived that the 'risen' Jesus was or had been the subject of anything else but Jewish individual resurrection, which he had!

What most sceptics fail to realise when they argue against the Resurrection is that it really happened . . . although in the Jewish form.

What their Pauline believing opponents fail to realise when they point to the empty tomb is that it was *not* empty, and even had it been, it wouldn't have amounted to a row of pins because there was Jesus outside and there was the '*gol*' rolled aside from the doorway.

And who were these 'angels' with radiant faces and shining white garments? As we dismiss all supernatural manifestations as nonsense, we can see these 'angels' only as men. What men?

From their dress of shining white—the normal non-working habits of the Essenes—we can see these men only as members of that sect.

There is no longer any doubt that a plot to save Jesus from the Cross *did* exist, probably along the lines already predicated; therefore some form of medical attention would have been provided the moment the badly beaten, drugged, and certainly deeply shocked King of the Jews was removed from the scaffold and had reached the privacy of the tomb.

A Roman physician would have imposed an impossible risk; the imminence of the Sabbath would have prevented any orthodox Jewish physician from touching a crucified man without defiling himself, so what was left? Only the Essenes, some of whom were reputed to have been highly skilled in therapeutics; moreover, having eaten their Paschal Feast two nights before, they were under no risk of defilement.

It is probable that the first of these angels in white crept into the commodious tomb on Friday while the crowd's attention was focussed on the Cross.

Swiftly wrapping the naked Jesus in a sheet, Joseph of Arimathea and Nicodemus carried him into the tomb, allegedly wrapped him in myrrh and aloes—'about an hundred pound weight'—and departed, rolling the stone 'go!' to seal the entrance and left Jesus all alone ... but for the waiting, hidden physician.

That 'hundred pound weight' of spices worries us. This was a greatly excessive quantity, which would have filled a large sack, brought to the tomb by Nicodemus, probably on the back of a donkey. In view of the absurd amount we are, perhaps, entitled to think that other things might have been concealed in that sack beneath a top layer of herbs; other things such as a physician might need, as well as sandals and the shining white raiment needed to transform a naked King into a living Essene.

When Mary looked into the 'empty' tomb at first light on Sunday with Peter at her side, they were able to give a rather minute description of its contents and condition. They saw the linen swathing sheet lying on the shelf and the head napkin neatly folded. It is strange that neither apparently saw that 'hundred pound weight' of myrrh and aloes either on the shelf or spilled on the floor. Such a large quantity could not have been missed ... if ever it was there.

When, later, Mary mistook a man for the gardener and suddenly realised it was Jesus, what was he wearing? Naked he had entered the tomb and, unless someone other than a providential God, who thinks of everything, had provided him with clothing, naked he emerged. So where did it come from? From Nicodemus' sack of goodies?

What Jew in his right mind would provide clothes for a dead man whose resurrection—in the Christian sense— was not only unexpected but unimaginable? But they would have been provided had there been even a slim hope that Jesus might have need for them ... and this makes it practically certain that he was not dead when removed from the Cross and had never intended to be.

As the gospels quite plainly report that the risen Jesus was both solid flesh and bone—and even invited doubters to feel that this was so, and ate solid food—and yet was entirely a spirit with the ability to 'float' through solid walls, why was the stone rolled from the entrance, which was also the exit? While nobody could get in while it was in position, it was even more certain that nobody could get out. If, then, Jesus were a spirit with the ability to materialise through stone walls, why was it necessary that the stone '*gol*' be moved? Commonsense suggests that it had to be moved—and from outside—because until it was, the two solid, living men inside simply couldn't escape from the tomb. The stone movers were probably more Essenes who were in the plot. Perhaps they had arrived later than planned . . . or Mary came earlier than expected, and saw what she wasn't wanted to see.

One feels that but for her embarrassing arrival Jesus would simply have vanished, leaving everyone to imagine—as they had at first—that tomb robbers had been at work. However, discovered by his wife just as he was about to vanish into the early morning mist of the Lower Kidron Valley, there was little else that he could do but bluff things out. Pretending at first to be the gardener, his great love for his wife proved too strong for his resolve merely to vanish and it was then that he uttered the heart-rending 'Mary. . . !'

Now forced to modify his plans and, perhaps, feeling secure in his disguise—which might have included the shaving-off of his beard—Jesus decided on a last meeting with his friends and disciples before he finally 'vanished'.

This done and arrangements made for Mary and Jesus bar Abbas—he had already provided for his mother when on the Cross—he allowed a chosen few to accompany him a little of the way, exchanged last greetings . . . and ascended a hill and was gone.

Keeping in mind that he partook of the Passover Feast with a group of Essenes in their own quarter of Jerusalem and, we say, was aided by them in his successful bid to cheat the Cross where, after he vanished from his disciples' sight, is he likely to have gone?

If the Kidron Valley in which, we say, that tomb still stands, is followed until it becomes the Lower Kidron and eventually turns east and becomes a deep *wadi*, its twists and turns will eventually bring one out on the western shore of the Dead Sea . . . at Qumran, the settlement of the Essenes. And there, although there is no proof—unless it exists in the scroll written by Jesus of Gennesareth—the gospel Jesus who was King of Israel passed the rest of his days, possibly with his beloved Mary. Perhaps only a discreet few knew his secret and, perhaps, he watched in cynical silence as a man named Saul slowly but surely turned his miraculous escape from the Cross into the Resurrection and went on from that to evolve his breathtaking but thoroughly pagan-to-Jesus concept of Man's relationship to God.

And so, ironically, as an Essene monk, Jesus might have written parchments extolling the only true God—JHWH of Israel—while he was slowly turned into the Son of that God, which would have shocked him to the very depths of his Jewish soul.

And so the years could have passed, placidly, until whispers grew into mutters and finally became the roar of a people in rebellion. Deciding on one final toss of the dice, the Hasmoneans assembled their meagre forces and marched on to destiny . . . and Masada.

The year was 66 A.D.

20 / The Skeletons in the Cave

Masada is a place of dark, brooding secrets! Even standing at its foot, with its crumbling brown bulk rearing starkly and almost vertically a quarter of a mile overhead, it grips the imagination with forebodings of evil. Here, the past is either incredibly distant . . . or unbearably close.

You lean on a rock wall and discover that it is the perimeter defence of a Roman camp, looking just as it did when the 'legio Fretensis'—the 'Bloody X Legion'—had marched out through that gateway beside you and along the Dead Sea shore precisely 1900 years ago. There's another camp behind you . . . more of them in the hills above; the refuse of history but still in perfect condition to

Once part of the Wilderness of Judea, the flat-topped

be used if ever the Legions came this way again.

mountain has been severed from the plateau by a gigantic wadi which slashes behind it, playing the gashed throat to Masada's bleeding head. The illusion is complete when the late afternoon sun, filtered by the desert dust, paints the scene the colour of blood . . . reminding one that there was a day when this was only too literally true.

Even before you're told that prehistoric man's artifacts have been found in its caves, one instinctively feels that Masada must have played a significant role in primitive Canaan's superstitions and religion. It's that sort of mountain. It just crouches there . . . and waits.

One recalls the long Persian domination of this land and thinks of the great burning fires of Zoroastrianism—whose last dying embers still glow in the devotions of the Parsees of India—and wonders was this, perhaps, ever a shrine to the Zoroastrian fire god Mazda . . . and was the mountain named in his honour.

Masada was one of the very first pieces of Hasmonean real estate to fall like a fat, ripe plum into Herod the Great's greedy paw. Improving on the former King's fortifications Herod turned it into an impregnable fortress of elaborate luxury, giving it a large, permanent garrison and packing its cavernous store rooms to bulging with so much food and arms that even almost seventy years after his death, there was more than enough of both to support three thousand fighting Jews and their wives and children for seven years.

One wonders why Herod had gone to this enormous trouble for the stronghold can never have been of any great strategic importance, and surveyed little else but the myriads of scuttling scorpions in the wadis below. Josephus, however, clears up the mystery; Masada was Herod's bolt-hole: 'In case of danger from the Jewish masses, who might push him off his throne and *restore to power the royal house that had preceded him!*' How more significant can an historical comment be than that?

The state of the country and the temper of the Hasmonean Zealots can't better be described and all that remains to be added is that for seventy years after the Butcher of Bethlehem's death, Rome maintained a large garrison at Masada ... in order to deny its use to the Hasmoneans.

They bided their time until 66 A.D. then struck!

In short time the Romans were booted out of the fortress and the Zealots took over. Then, in what seems to have been a unilateral and totally unauthorised act of opportunism, Mennahem—a grandson of Judas the Galilean who had raided Sepphoris shortly after the presumed birth of Jesus—left the main Zealot force at Masada and with a few supporters, marched to Jerusalem, which 'he entered like a King!'

Clearly, here was another Hasmonean making his bid but, unfortunately for Mennahem, all that came off was his foolish head. The survivors drifted back to Masada led by the ill-fated 'king's' kinsman, Eleazar ben Ja'ir, of whom more will be told. This Eleazar was to command the fortress and its three thousand inhabitants for seven incredible years while the whole country burst into a flaming war with Rome, caused by the very act of the Zealot's seizure of Masada.

That this was merely the opening overt action in a powerful struggle to restore the Hasmoneans needs no proof, for the facts speak for themselves. The thing which baffles historians, however, is why the Zealots of Masada took no further part in the war which raged for seven years. Instead, they idled here in their eyrie gazing stolidly at the tideless, sterile waters of the Dead Sea for the four years it took the Romans to subdue all Israel, then quite unemotionally watched for another three years while the Romans prepared to winkle them out of Masada. They needed every last day of it, too!

It was to the safety of Masada that a trickle of refugees from the Essene community at Qumran had fled in 68 A.D. when, in a rare and astonishing Roman act of violence against Judaism, General Vespasian actually broke off the siege of Jerusalem in order to attack the settlement and massacre most of the 'harmless' Essenes.

Why?

At the most, Rome had offered only pinpricks against Judaism in one hundred years and, for most of this time, was most tolerant. Now, without known provocation or reason, came this bloody slaughter of the sectarians who produced the Dead Sea Scrolls. Does the explanation lie in the fact that the Essenes might not have been quite as inoffensive as they were reputed to have been? It is a fact of recorded history that General—later Emperor—Vespasian had early realised that the rebellion wouldn't subside until he damped down the fires of Hebrew nationalism and Messianism by completing the sadly botched work of Herod and killed off the very last Hasmonean. Was his attack on Qumran an indication that he thought the Essenes were up to their sanctified necks in the rebellion just as much as the Zealots were? Or did he, perhaps, hear a certain rumour and decide to run down the truth of it?

Two years after the Qumran horror the bulk of the rebels moved at last to intervene in the fight for Jerusalem, leaving about one thousand fighting-men and their women and children behind at Masada. Why? Why did this garrison stay? Already the military situation was quite hopeless; the rebellion had failed and the Holy City as good as fallen yet . . . they stayed.

Another two years went by and theirs was the only point of armed resistance left in all Israel. They were doomed . . . and knew it, yet they stayed.

They watched unmoved while the Romans came and, under General Flavius Silva, built an immense stone wall of *circumvallation*—still to be seen—running up mountains and down chasms like some monstrous boa-constrictor, until its head swallowed its tail and the ring of death was complete. They were sheep for the slaughter and safely in the fold.

On 14 April 73 A.D. and after three years of prodigious effort, the exultant Romans knew that the fortress was theirs, or would be on the morrow. Working from the top of a gigantic rock and timber tower plated with sheets of iron, and resting on an earthen ramp which they had filled a whole *valley* to construct, they smashed away at the gates with an enormous battering ram. For days it had been at its monotonous work until now, on this mid-April day, the wall was breached in the afternoon.

To their dismay, the Romans found that the wily Zealots had built an earth and timber barricade at this very spot; it would have to be destroyed before the swords could go to work. Setting fire to it with flaming pitch regurgitated from the Dead Sea, the Legionaries retired down to their camps and left the flames to do the hard work.

During the hours of darkness—perhaps soon after midnight—guards raised the alarm: 'Fire!' Gazing up, the troops could see a great red glow suffusing the mountain top, but thinking that the burning barricade had merely spread a bit, the tired Romans went back to sleep.

When they bridged the gap between their tower and Masada's broken wall next morning, the fortress was strangely silent, and its stubborn Jewish defenders invisible. Covered by a hundred archers in case of a trap, the first assault troops crept inside. They were met by a scene of horror!

Wherever they looked, the ground was littered with corpses of men, women and children, each with its ghastly wound. From what was left of the buildings, sullen smoke drifted as the last combustibles were turned to ashes. Over everything there hung a terrible silence, made more awful as it was broken by the crashing of a charred beam. Otherwise, no voice was to be heard; no dog barked; no child laughed or whimpered and even the birds were gone. There was nothing but the bloody bodies, the charred ruins, drifting smoke ... and the awful silence of death, which not even the Romans dared break by shouting.

Some time during that night of horror the Zealots of Masada had ended their strange seven-years-long vigil.

Putting the buildings to the torch, they had appointed a squad of executioners and quietly bared their breasts to the Holy Swords of Israel.

While a whole Roman Legion had slept like snoring pigs in their camps below ... 965 men, women and children had died in the night, in silent and superb contempt for the enemies of Israel.

And that, according to Flavius Josephus who is our only, though not our most reliable, witness is the story of the epic at Masada. But is it true?

In posing the question, no insult is offered to the valiant Jewish thousand who died upon Masada that night and whose chilling sacrifice has evoked the admiration and compassion of millions, and will continue to do so. Such is the fierce pride those deaths have engendered in Jews the whole world over that, in Israel, the armed forces come to Masada to swear fealty to the Star of David on the blood-drenched soil of the sacred mountain, and to vow that 'Masada Shall Not Fall Again'! Verily I say, the spirit of Judah ha-Makkabah is still abroad in the land of Israel!

But the truth? What is it?

The suspected truth could be even more glorious than that accepted, for it is probable that the devious Josephus told only part of the epic story and, like the bad Hasmonean he was, concealed the rest.

This, if true, spins a golden thread of glory which even the proudest of nations will envy.

*　　*　　*

Incredible though it seems, Masada was actually 'lost' for some one thousand two hundred years.

When, somewhere about 600 A.D. the invading Arabs defeated the Christian Byzantines—inheritors from Rome—the black pall of Mohammedanism descended like a long night over quivering Israel and hid Masada from the eyes of the Christian west for almost fifty generations. Soon, men forgot about the lonely mountain by the Dead Sea, and, after a time, it was largely thought that no such place had ever existed; that Masada was in the same category as legendary Camelot and, as such, was a figment of Josephus' fertile imagination.

Then came the Americans to the Holy Land and, in 1838, one of them spotted what he thought was a house

of some kind on the rocky outcrop of a gnarled, cinna-
mon-brown mountain by the Dead Sea. Masada had been
found.

Many were to scratch around the ruins during the next
century—awed by what they saw—but it was not until
1963 that the Government of Israel determined to ex-
cavate the site, as much to test the truth of Josephus' account as to reveal the past.

And so was set up the first really scientific archaeological expedition to probe Masada's secrets, under the leadership of General-Professor Yigael Yadin, the noted Israeli
soldier, patriot and scholar.

Exciting even before a spade was plunged into the historic soil, the expedition's first discoveries—quickly made—
were even more so and helped place Masada high on the
archaeological exploration honours list, not only for the
quantity, variety and quality of the relics recovered, but
for the speed of their discovery.

Earthquakes had contrived what the time and weather
of nineteen centuries had been unable to effect in the bone
dry climate of the Wilderness of Judea. Almost all of the
numerous buildings which liberally littered the boat-shaped
mountain top ʾand had made it a showplace in King Herod's day, were now just piles of tumbled masonry. The
treasures lay beneath.

Not only were ancient parchment scrolls found, but
coins, tools, weapons, catapult ammunition, wine jars,
beads, rings, buckles, jewellery, cosmetics, ovens, pots and
pans, ready-set fires with fresh fuel alongside, lamps,
dishes, food, baskets and even remnants of woven fabric
clothing. In many cases, their survival was incredible.

The absolute wonder of it all was that it had all happened long before there had been anything called the New
World, and when the peoples of much of Europe—and all
of Britain—had been little more than howling, blue-painted
savages 'running on all fours'. Here, where God had
been the personal possession of perhaps four or five million people tucked away in this tiny Mediterranean back-
water, a culture had flourished; a culture of such wisdom
and merciful justice that some modern nations have not
yet achieved. Now, on this day in the sixties of the present
century, it was possible for many a Jew of this expedition
to stoop and pick up a remnant of a woven tunic that

might have been worn by his direct ancestor almost two thousand years before. Oh, the wonder of it all!

However, of all the Masada Expedition's discoveries none could possibly have been more dramatic or moving to the men who found them than two separate finds at opposite ends of the plateau.

In the ruins of what had once been the tiled floor bathroom of the mighty Herod the Great's fabulous 'hanging' palace at the northern end—the grooves worn by his buttocks sliding over the bath's high side still visible—the excavators came upon tragic evidence of what must have happened in this place.

And, remember, we are talking about real people who had lived—and died—only a few years after the events that had involved Jesus. Many of them or their fathers must have heard him; some might even have known him.

On the mosaic floor of this room whose walls still bore the sinister stains of spilled blood, were the skeletal remains of a young man and woman and, presumably, their child. Lying there in the shambles of arrowheads and silver scales of armour from the jerkin, were the remains of at least three of the valiant 965 who had died on that distant night. With them were the lady's leather sandals, scarcely less fashionable than any to be seen on the smart beaches of Tel-Aviv or Haifa today.

Most astounding and moving of all ... her scalp, covered with brown hair still neatly braided into plaits whose still visible sheen suggested that her coiffure had been completed only a few days before ... and yet it was two thousand years ago. The effect of this relic on the men of Israel must have been both terrible ... and wonderful, and a great tenderness for the unknown lady who had braided her hair so neatly must have flooded through them all.

The group of excavators must have recalled Josephus' description of the last few minutes before the final few themselves fled into eternity: 'And he who was the last of all, took a view of all the other bodies . . . and when he perceived that all were slain, he set fire to the palace and, with the force of his hand ran his sword entirely through himself, and fell down dead near to his own relations.'

Had the archaeologists discovered the remains of the Masada Commander, Eleazar ben Ja'ir, and his wife and child? Although the man's age—the early twenties—seems against the identification, all Jewish males were adult men at 13 and most were fathers five years later. If Eleazar were a person of importance—and he was actually of astonishing importance, as will be shown at the proper time—there is no reason why he should not have been in command at such a 'tender' age, particularly if he inherited the position in an emergency. Remember that Alexander the Great had conquered half the then-known world before he was thirty!

Travelling now to the opposite end of the plateau, we find this to be the barest and most deserted part of the fortress complex. Few buildings were ever erected here and though Herod's double casemated wall encloses the whole perimeter at the very edge of the plateau, this part of his domain was apparently devoted to little more than several ancient graveyards which, though possibly invisible from the ground, are plainly discernible in aerial photographs.

Wishing to investigate some caves high in the face of the southernmost cliff below the top, the archaeologists made a perilous descent by ropes, entered one of the caves ... and stopped dead in their tracks.

Lying in the ancient dust and shrouded by the wind-blown debris of twenty centuries, lay a group of twenty-five skeletons.

Examined later by Dr. N. Hass of the Hebrew University Medical School, they definitely proved to have been those of some of Masada's defenders. Fourteen were males aged between 22 and 60; one had been a man of between 70 and 80; six were females between 15 and 22, and four were of children of from 8 to 12 years old. There was also a foetus!

Who were these people?

Why, out of 965 men, women and children who died on the night of 14 April 73 A.D., were these the only remains discovered, apart from the Eleazar trio?

What happened to the others?

With nearly a thousand bodies to dispose of, what else are the Romans likely to have done but merely toss them over the edge of the precipices to crash in the chasms below? Probably this wasn't done in the case of Commander Eleazar and his little family as a tribute to his valour. But what of these others?

There are only two viable explanations: either the Romans were unaware of the bodies in the cave or, knowing of them, they let these, too, lie undisturbed for the very same reason. But why and how did they merit this tribute from Rome?

The theory that these twenty-five comprised a representative sample of Masada's defenders seems unlikely to be correct. As an extreme argument against it, what was the man of well over 70 doing at Masada? He could scarcely have been a warrior at that age, so what was he doing there at all?

And the women? Had these women been here at Masada for seven years—as they had—then the eldest in the group must have arrived aged 15, the age of marriage. Where were her children? Though the foetus might have been hers, where were the other five or six she would have had over this time? The youngest of the children found, was 8 and the oldest, 12, so that it is obvious that none could have been born at Masada, which is remarkable. So, too, is the fact that though all these women were of marriageable age, none of the children found could have belonged to any of them nor, apparently, did they have any of their own.

What we are really being asked to accept is that these six women, who had spent seven years on Masada among a probable six hundred virile, sex-starved fighting-men with little to do but watch the girls, had had only one child between them—and that unborn—in a span of seven whole years? Probability just won't stretch that far!

The suggestion that this group of twenty-five were left unmolested where they fell simply because the Romans were unaware of their existence, also seems highly improbable. We know that the Roman troops searched Masada's nooks and crannies with 'a fine tooth-comb' and, in fact and as Josephus reports, actually found two women and three children hiding unscathed somewhere on the mountain. In the circumstances, it is unlikely that they left these caves at the southern end unsearched, particularly as they are clearly visible from at least two of the camps close by.

On the evidence, it seems reasonable to suggest that these were a very special twenty-five people and that General Silva accorded them exactly the same accolade as was given to Eleazar ben Ja'ir . . . and let them lie where they had fallen under the swords of the Zealot executioners.

There can have been only one reason why.

The Roman General must have known them to comprise a special group deserving of special treatment, but what group?

It is in the answer to this question that the riddle's solution appears to lie . . . shocking to the devout of Christianity though it may be.

21 / The Enigma's Shocking Solution

The very first question which should have been asked about the Zealot's presence at Masada—but apparently was not—is: why were they there at all?

To accept the explanation of Josephus that they needed arms for Mennahem's bid for the throne, is to be content with only a part of the answer. This fails to explain why up to three thousand men, women and children had to scale the mountain merely to obtain arms; the men, yes ... but the others, no! And having obtained those weapons, why was it necessary for most of the three thousand to stay there for most of the next seven years, and a thousand of them for all that time? And during these seven years, while all these tough, well-armed troops idled their lives away, all Israel bled to death around them.

That they all were not enthusiastic supporters of Mennahem seems positive, for not only did but a 'handful' of Zealots go on the ill-fated venture to Jerusalem but, when it failed, the survivors returned to Masada and stayed there for at least another six years.

What was their object?

If we are correct in seeing the seizure of Masada as the spark which ignited the flames of war—whose object was the restoration of the Hasmonean throne—why did the Zealots remain there after their leader was dead? Even more interestingly, why did not the next inheritor step forward? We know that Eleazar ben Ja'ir was kinsman to Mennahem, so why did he not make his bid? That he did not suggests that there was another Hasmonean heir at Masada more senior than either Mennahem or Eleazar, and that the former might even have jumped the gun.

If so, why didn't this more senior claimant step forward? The suggestion is that he had already done so, and that it was his earlier bid for the throne that the war was really all about. This would define Mennahem's attempted coup as a revolt within a revolt and the fact that his 'reign' in Jerusalem was astonishingly brief and that he was actually deposed and put to death after a few days by a rival Hasmonean faction tends to reinforce that opinion.

Leaving this hidden claimant for the moment, let us now seek an answer to another intriguing question: why did the Romans lay siege to Masada?

At first look, it might seem that Josephus' reason is correct, but is it? He says: 'In Judea, Bassus (the Procurator) had died and the new Procurator was Flavius Silva who, seeing the rest of the countryside reduced to impotence and only one fortress holding out, marched against it with all available forces. The fortress was Masada, occupied by the *Sicarili* (shades of Judas the Sicarii) under the command of . . .' The rest, we know.

Should we accept the above account as correct?

General Vespasian having become Emperor of Rome, command of the Roman forces in Judea fell to his son, Titus—also, later, Emperor—who, with five Legions plus some ancillary troops such as cavalry, archers and sappers, flattened the fortified, mile-square Holy City defended by more than *a million* . . . in just *seven months!* Yet we are expected to believe that an entire Legion—the toughest and best Rome had; the Bloody X—one fifth of Titus' total forces, was sent to subdue an isolated fortress in the Wilderness of Judea, which at this stage, was defended by no more than some six hundred fighting-men. There can be no argument that this was what was done; what we contest is the reason *why* it was done.

There were—and still are—only two ways in or out of Masada. At the time of the siege, both were precipitous goat-tracks extremely difficult to negotiate in safety. Half a cohort—about two hundred and fifty men—could have sealed them both off efficiently and completely effectively, yet the Procurator of all Judea took over personal command of the crack X legion from Larcius Lepidus and led the sweating, cursing 6,000 veterans, plus 15,000 Jewish prisoners, out into the oven that was the desert, with every prospect of an indefinite stay. Here, where food and water had to be hauled many miles every few days, the Legion slaved like coolies alongside the prisoners, building that immense enclosing wall, filling in a valley and building a gigantic 150 foot high assault tower—and took three years doing all that—apparently so they could eventually face the defenders eyeball to eyeball. This is really all it amounted to for, in the event, the Roman troops never even wet a sword.

There must have been some other awfully compelling reason for all this long, hard, prodigiously expensive and even desperate campaign. Josephus' reason just isn't good enough.

So we are faced with a triplet of questions: why were the Zealots at Masada?; why did no Hasmonean claimant step forward on the death of Mennahem?; why did the Romans go to such Herculean lengths to get at 600 Zealot troops? To this list we add a fourth which, perhaps, is the key to the whole mystery: why did the Zealots virtually commit suicide on the night of 14 April A.D. 73?

Nearly eighty generations have unquestioningly accepted the explanation that self-destruction was the garrison's preferred alternative to falling into the hands of the Romans, yet this is seriously to be doubted. Although the Romans dealt savagely with some prisoners and often ruthlessly massacred whole villages and towns, this was more often than not the result of Jewish treachery or intransigence; there are just as many examples of Roman generosity to the defeated and, indeed, Josephus was himself a living example. This being so, there seems little doubt that at least up to the time the battering ram set to work, the garrison would have had little trouble in negotiating a generous surrender ... had they merely been what they are said to have been, rebels. That they did not attempt to bargain but 'preferred' to die seems to indicate much more than a sudden loss of fighting spirit.

When one remembers that the Zealots were renowned last-ditch fighters, their collapse seems even more inexplicable until one also remembers that the Zealots were actually religious militants; Josephus called them Israel's fourth estate, counting them after the Pharisees, Sadducees, and the Essenes.

Having sprung from the rigidly religious Maccabees and being dedicated to that family's religious rule, their sudden collapse and self-destruction might have been due to a revival of the original Maccabean refusal to contravene God's Law by fighting on the Sabbath.

We know that although Judas Maccabeus discarded the prohibition on the score of expediency, it was later reestablished. When Pompey attacked Jerusalem at about 60

B.C. and a century before Masada, he very quickly discovered that the easiest road to victory lay in attacking only on the Jewish Sabbath, when he was permitted to batter away at the walls with no hand lifted against him.

So that it seems likely that the Zealots were more in fear of the calendar than of the Romans.

It was late afternoon when Masada's wall was breached. Disliking night fighting, which they regarded as impossible in the darkness, the Romans withdrew until the morrow. However, a few minutes after they did so, the sun set and a new Jewish day commenced ... which might have been the Sabbath! Unable on this day to fight or treat for surrender, the Zealots faced certain butchery at dawn.

This, in fact, is the very implication contained in the 'fifteenth' scroll found at Masada whose author, Jesus of Gennesareth, wrote that the Romans broke down the wall 'on the eve of the Sabbath'. Why mention the fact unless it played a significant part in the events which followed?

Having now got the scroll author 'onstage' we find that he has made the perfect entrance for it is he who is believed to be the answer to all three questions concerning Masada: why were the Zealots there?; why did no further Hasmonean claimant step forward? and why did the Romans go to such fantastic extremes to capture the place?

This Jesus of Gennesareth claimed to have been the last of the Hasmonean Kings of Israel, meaning in real terms that he was the heir to the throne—which did not exist—and would occupy it in the event of a restoration, which would do much more than re-establish the former dynasty; it would bring about the virtual Kingdom of God on Earth ... which is precisely what another Jesus is reputed to have sought to bring about.

The Zealots were at Masada, we say, because they constituted a royal bodyguard about the family and person of the Hasmonean heir, who was the scroll author, Jesus of Gennesareth. Masada had been seized in his name in 66 A.D., while he might have been somewhere else—such as Qumran—incognito, but knowing full well that his secret must get out and that one day the vengeance of Rome would be swift and bloody. It was against this day that another, and a safer refuge, would be needed that Masada was first seized. Taking advantage of the true heir's absence, the faithless Mennahem tried to seize power for himself, and died.

Eventually, in 68 A.D. came the day Jesus of Gennesareth had foreseen two years before, the Romans struck at Qumran and, just before they did, the heir of the Hasmoneans slipped south to Masada, where everything awaited his coming. Again, the Zealots swarmed around the 'queen-bee' who was, this time, a king.

Either the Romans thought that they had got their man in the Qumran massacre or, realising that he'd evaded them and suspecting he was at Masada, they put aside all plans of seizing him until the fall of Jerusalem. True or not, the fact is that they made no move against the fortress until the Holy City was taken.

Knowing the history of Judea almost as well as did the Jews, the Romans would have been well aware that Masada had been a Hasmonean refuge for two centuries before the times of Herod the Great; that it had so served him and was now almost certainly being used by another Hasmonean 'king' who was surrounded by six hundred fanatics sworn to defend him with their lives.

If we are correct in seeing the scroll author Jesus of Gennesareth, as this Hasmonean king, we must also see him as the Jewish Messiah-elect, which is how the Zealots must have seen him and, possibly, the rest of the nation, too. The Jews were certainly fighting against Rome, but if it were not for this potential King, what were they fighting *for*? If not for him, for what else? There was nothing. Without a cause, the rebellion and war seems to have been pointless and yet, there was the whole land a-rattle with battle from one end to the other. There had to be a reason for the Jews having started the war and it would be absurd, in the circumstances, not to believe that the restoration was it.

This was certainly so with the Zealots who, having sworn to defend to the death their King-Messiah, who was the anointed of God, would scarcely have broken God's Law by fighting on the Sabbath. As the calendar thus made death mandatory, they saw it more acceptable both to God and themselves that the swords they were to die under were their own rather than Roman.

And so it must have been decided by Jesus of Gennesareth as the Sabbath began, and his awful decision con-

veyed to the people by the Commander—and his kin—
Eleazar ben Ja'ir.

According to Josephus, lots were chosen to select ten
men who, with Eleazar at their head, would that night
slay every man, woman and child on Masada.

Amazingly enough, the story about the eleven lots was
confirmed when the archaeologists discovered in the shambles around what had been the command-post, eleven
shards of pottery each inscribed with a man's name ...
one of them actually 'Eleazar ben Ja'ir', probably in his
own hand-writing.

Lots chosen and tossed to the ground, the ten went
about their awful duty. We are told that whole families
lay down alongside each other and calmly bared their
breasts to the sword.

Probably as the common folk of Masada were dying
ten at a time, Eleazar ben Ja'ir shepherded the Royal
Family of young and old to the cave at the southern end
of the plateau. If they had to die, at least here they might
lie in some privacy and dignity. A solemn muttered
prayer, and then Eleazar put them to death as swiftly and
as painlessly as possible.

His terrible task done, Eleazar must carefully have in-
spected that other place of carnage and, seeing that all
were dead and the buildings afire as ordered, went to meet
the ten who, in their turn, submitted to his weary sword.

His task still not fully done, he slowly went towards Herod the Great's villa hanging on an outcrop below the
summit, where his young wife and son awaited his coming
... and Death awaited them all.

A possible objection to the suggestion that the twenty-
five members of the Hasmonean Royal Family were killed
in the cave is the difficulty experienced by the archaeologists in reaching it. How had women and children, and the
old man of over 70 managed? Obviously, in 73 A.D. there
had been an easier access, since eroded away; had there
not been and they had not gone alive to the cave, their
bodies would have presented even more difficulties for the
Zealot executioners than was experienced by the living archaeologists. However, if they were killed in some other
spot and their bodies lowered by ropes to the cave, this
makes the suggestion that they comprised a very special
group that much more persuasive, and likely.

That some suspicion of their identity might have been

held by the Israel Government Department of Antiquities—under whose aegis the Archaeological Expedition was mounted—seems to be indicated by the twenty-five 'skeletons' strange subsequent history.

Although discovered late in 1963 or early in 1964 and the Jewish Rabbinate was anxious at that early time to accord them proper religious burial, the remains were kept above ground—although treated with the utmost respect—for a period of six years until July 1969. Although there probably exists some very good reason for the delay, it seems strange in view of the Jewish Rabbinate's anxiety, that it should have lasted so long.

With full military honours, the twenty-eight heroes of Masada—the foetus not being counted—were laid to rest in a common grave at the mountain's foot, one thousand nine hundred years after their tragic, noble deaths on Masada.

If these sad bones were all that remained of the Hasmonean Royal Family, it seems altogether impossible not to identify the patriach of over seventy as the author of the scroll handled at Lod Airport that night in 1964, the mysterious Jesus of Gennesareth who described himself as 'son of nearly eighty years', and also as 'the last Hasmonean King of Israel' and thus, the Messiah.

Was he, at the same time, something more?

Earlier reference was made to a particularly important bearing which Masada's Commander, Eleazar ben Ja'ir, might have on this investigation. It lies in his good wholesome Hebrew name which, however, is most unusual and is met with on only two occasions outside the writings of Flavius Josephus.

Ja'ir was the name borne by one of Israel's early Judges or tribal chiefs who ruled the ancient Hebrews before the days of great and glorious King David. In its Greek form of '*Jairus*' it is also found in the Christian gospels, Jairus being the name of the Ruler of the Synagogue at Capernaum whose little daughter is said to have been raised from the dead ... by Jesus!

To find what must have been a grandson of this same Jairus—whose family must ever after have borne an undischargable obligation to Jesus—serving as Commander of the Masada garrison of Zealots who had sworn to guard the life of 'Jesus of Gennesareth' with their own, is a coincidence of such astonishing magnitude that it might not be one.

Another astonishing footnote is provided by one of the best preserved of Masada's buildings, the remains of a Christian Church built sometime about the 4th century by monks of the Byzantine Chruch in Constantinople. Here, amid the already ruined palaces of Herod the Great and the pathetic relics of the Jewish heroes' tragic sacrifice, these Christian monks elected to build their tiny church. Here they lived and worshipped Jesus of Nazareth for almost five hundred years . . . and then they vanished.

Byzantine monks swarmed into Palestine (Judea) when Christianity became the official religion of the Roman Empire in 323 A.D. and built many such churches and monasteries throughout the land. Invariably these were sited at places regarded—however incorrectly—as sacred to Christian traditions because of their association with Jesus of Nazareth.

Why, then, did they build such a church here on Masada, which is not supposed to have had the slightest association with him or even with the very early Nazarean-Christian Church?

Despite this, they very clearly regarded this as a sacred site.

Why?

The answer to that question must remain an awful hook of anguish for Christians . . . as, too, must that grave at Masada's foot.

So, with our detective story almost complete, we ask was the bogus 'Professor Max Grosset' really right, after all? That question will have to be answered by each of us in his own way and according to what he believes . . . or does not.

Perhaps 'Jesus of Gennesareth' and his 'fifteenth' scroll was a fake and a hoax, and Professor Grosset mad.

Perhaps.

However, if it were so, it seems extraordinary how his 'impossible' identification of the scroll author and that document's claims have been so strongly supported by historical research . . . and even by the gospels themselves.

What is the answer to that, one wonders?

And the scroll? Where is it now?

As the full story of the present author's involvement is detailed in the following Appendix, all that need be said here is that strong circumstantial evidence exists that it is—or was—inside the Soviet Union, and that its existence is already known to the senior hierarchy of the Christian Church, as are its contents.

Early in February 1967, an astonishing event occurred! Suddenly the fifty years wide chasm of enmity and mutual bitterness between the Vatican and the Kremlin was dramatically bridged by Premier Podgorny of the U.S.S.R. who requested—and was granted—an urgent audience with His Holiness, Pope Paul.

The details of that meeting have never been revealed nor has even a hint of what it was about ever been so much as whispered to an astounded, incredulous world.

The likelihood that the audience could have concerned the Russian Premier's immortal soul is thought to be rather too remote to be considered and, while it might have been confined to politics—the main preoccupation of the Church, if not its vocation—the suspicion exists that it might have been at this astonishing meeting that His Holiness first heard of the 'fifteenth' scroll and of Jesus of Gennesareth.

By an altogether curious coincidence, very soon after this meeting there came a complete about-face in the public relations of the Church vis-a-vis the Kremlin. Not only in Russia but even in its satellite countries Anti-Christ seemed to have been toppled as the Press fell over itself to be the first to praise the Catholic Church. After fifty years of vilification, suddenly all was sunshine and smiles. Why?

Rome's tit for Moscow's tat was soon to be revealed. The Vatican actually came out solidly in support for the Moslems in their bitter quarrel with Israel, which might have seemed strange to some until it was recalled that *Moslem* Egypt, *Moslem* Syria, *Moslem* Jordan and a few *Moslem* others were the Arab States' allies in the famous six-day war with Israel, and all were backed with Soviet Union arms and, undoubtedly, were embarked on a course that brought smiles in the Kremlin.

Why would the Vatican indulge in such folly?

It is suggested that the Vatican could not help itself. All it could do to put a little chocolate on the bitter pill of partisanship was release the Jews from almost twenty centuries of guilt for the part their ancestors were alleged to have played in the death of Jesus of Nazareth.

Why? And why, just at that time?

Was it due to any sudden doubt as to how and when the historical Jesus had actually died?

And so, you see, there is more than a chance that the curious old parchment written by the hand of Jesus of Gennesareth all those centuries ago, might well represent a veritable 'time-bomb' that is ticking away the final hours of the Christian Faith . . . as we know it, or think we do.

Again we remind you of that Dean of St. Paul's who, a decade ago—and who was therefore speaking in a different context—said: 'I see no reason to suppose that a complete abandonment of the historical basis for Christianity would necessarily involve the end of the religion.'

Strangely enough, the very Apostle whose name is borne by the Dean's Cathedral, himself wrote: 'Hold fast to what is good!' He did not say, be it noted, that one should hold fast to what is *true!*

In that one fact might lie the real secret of the whole Christian ethic. One day, someone will try it out and, if it works, who knows where it might lead the world?

Appendix

The dialogue quoted in this section dealing with the emergence of the scroll in 1964 is not necessarily verbatim but, to the extent that it is, comes from notes made within a week of the event. The balance is as near as can be recalled and, if not exactly the dialogue of the occasion, certainly reflects the tenor of the conversation during the events.

Smuggling As an Art Form

Intent on writing an historical novel set in and around events in Judea in the late 1st century A.D.—with heavy emphasis on Masada—I wrote to General Yigael Yadin very early in November 1964 seeking a permit (if needed) to visit the excavations and, thinking this an automatic courtesy that would be granted any writer, went to New York to arrange publication with William Morrow & Company. That done, I arrived at Tel-Aviv's Lod Airport on the night of Thursday 3 December and within an hour was sitting in the lounge of the Dan Hotel, having a drink with 'Professor Max Grosset'.

Strangers until that hour, we introduced ourselves as I sat down at his table, the least busily occupied. Tongues wagging, he volunteered that he had the Chair of Semitic Languages & Studies at (mumble) University in the U.S.A. He intrigued one immediately because, though apparently working in America, he seemed to be a normal, well-bred Englishman; very tweedy and, with his shock of brown hair, bushy beard and thick lensed glasses, a crossbreeding of owl and teddybear.

When he heard that I was a writer he asked my interest in Israel and I blush to recall that I launched into an enthusiastic account of the Masada epic. He let me dangle over the pit awhile before letting me know that, earlier in the year, he had been a member of the Yigael Yadin Expedition.

Discovering that I hadn't, as yet, received a permit to visit the ruins, he became a prophet of gloom by predicting that I wouldn't be allowed to set foot on Masada. 'There are two reasons,' he said, when I demanded to know why, 'but the first is good enough to get you shot down in flames; you're a writer!' Adding that I should use my skull, forget Masada and catch the next plane home, he wandered off to the golden elevators, leaving me stunned.

Less than eighty-four hours later his prediction came true with a bang! Through his wife and secretary, General Yadin explained by letter that he had not received my application—airmailed a month before—until the day of my arrival. The staff being 'too busy to show you around', I was told that there would be no permit for me; instead, I was advised to buy a copy (35 cents) of the 31 October issue of the *Illustrated London News* which would tell me 'all I wanted to know.'

Fuming, I went to Jerusalem next day and rang Mrs. Yadin. She spoke excellent English but appeared tense. Pleading with her to ask her husband to reverse his decision, I explained that no 35 cent magazine could convey the feel of the textures, the smell of the earth or convey any really useful part of Masada's atmosphere and that only by immersing myself in all these things could I faithfully depict the fortress in my proposed book. Unless the decision was reversed, I said, my visit was aborted and my book stillborn. In short, my time and—even more importantly—my money should have been wasted.

'The more fool you,' said the lady icily. 'Anyway, you're supposed to be a writer; why don't you use your imagination?'

Sickened by this and suspecting there was more behind her attitude than sheer hostility, I bitchily suggested that they had found something important which they didn't want a writer to know about and stressed that I wasn't a journalist. Anyway, I half believed this to be true for I couldn't think of another possible reason. My remark earned an amazing reaction. Yelling into the phone that I must stop badgering her, the General's lady hung up in my ear.

Later that day I had an appointment at the Knesset—Israel's Parliament House—with Mr. Menachem Begin, the heroic former leader of the 'Irgun', one of Israel's underground armies during the War of Independence. At the present time he is, I believe, leader of the Gahal Party and a Minister without Portfolio in Premier Golda Meir's cabinet. By a strange coincidence, Mr. Begin was already aware of the Masada *impasse* when I met him; how, would take too long to recount.

He was incredulous that I couldn't get a permit to visit the fortress. 'Anyone can go to Masada,' he stormed, 'anyone!' He thumped the table. 'You come here to write a book about Israel that can only be to Israel's good, and the Yadins say ... !' He called several other M.P.s to the table and swiftly outlined the situation. They agreed that the fastest way to cut the red tape unreeling from #47 Ramban Street was the direct intervention of the Prime Minister, the late Mr. Levi Eshkol. Then and there, Mennahem Begin bustled off to a phone. When he came back, all smiles, he announced that the P.M.'s secretary—Teddy somebody—had assured him that all would be well.

'We'll probably make it an army operation,' laughed Begin. 'You'll be picked up, probably by army helicopter, flown through the Negev (the southern desert) and landed right on top of Masada. Now, you go back to Tel-Aviv and wait for a call from me!'

Delighted and extremely grateful ... and very much cock-a-hoop, I drove back to the Dan Hotel and dutifully awaited the promised call. It never came, not the next day, or ever!

Now comes the cloak-and-dagger stuff. Early that morning, my toilet bowl appeared to have been stuffed up with a copy of the *Jerusalem Post*—how, by whom and when—I can only guess; certainly it must have been while I slept. Reporting this at the desk, I left for Jerusalem with the assurance that all would be fixed, immediately. When I got back that night, the matter had not been attended to ... and they had already moved my gear to another room whose key was pushed invitingly across the desk to me. Thinking no evil, I shoved the key in my pocket and went in search of some food. In the lounge I met Grosset.

It was only then that I learned that, from the very first minute of our meeting the night of my arrival six nights earlier, I had probably been under surveillance, though whether by the official Shin Beth (the Israeli Secret Service) or some less romantic arm of security, is unknown. From what has since transpired in Australia up until 1970, the Shin Beth is my bet!

The archaeologist twitted me about my Masada permit so I described the events of the day and my encounter with Mrs. Yadin. Grosset scowled but let me finish without interruption. And then he spoke. What he said was so very strange that it is best described in dialogue.

'I wish you hadn't said that to Mrs. Yadin,' he started off. 'I mean about them finding something.'

'Why not?' I challenged. 'How the hell do you know they haven't, anyway? There has to be some reason why I was banned ... and it certainly can't be over anything I've said, written or done. I'm not a political animal nor am I anti-Semitic ... so why? Menachem Begin told me that anyone can go there ... so why not me? It has to be because I'm a writer ... as you said,' I reminded him, 'last Thursday night! Why wouldn't they want a writer there when, apparently, they've already spilled their guts to the *Illustrated London News*? Now, suddenly, they've gone all coy. Why? It has to be because they've found something they *don't* want the world to know about. In fact,' I finished, 'the more I think about it the more I'm sure that my crack to Mrs. Phone-banger could be smack on target!'

'I still wish you hadn't said it,' he muttered.

'Why the hell should you?'

Grosset sat biting his lip, his eyes measuring me shrewdly, like a tailor . . . or an undertaker. 'Because they'll think I told you,' he said, at last.

It was an astonishing remark, with all kinds of implications. 'Told me? Told me what? What's to tell and how could you know what's going on down at Masada if you haven't been near the place for six months?'

His reply flattened me.

'I was there about three weeks ago,' he said. 'And now I wish to God I'd never seen the place!'

To a writer, gold is very definitely where you find it. So I said nothing ... just sat toying with my empty glass ... and waited. When, at last he spoke, I knew that I was about to hear a confession, I knew it!

'You're right, you know, Joyce ... and you're all sorts of a clever bastard for foxing it out ... but something *has* been found down there, although you're wrong in thinking that the Yadins know exactly what it is.'

'How could they bloody help knowing?'

'Because I didn't bloody tell them,' was his cool reply. 'You see, I was the finder! It was at the end of last season, in fact, the very last day of it. I was working alone and ... well, let's just say that I found something I didn't report.'

'Like what?' He looked hard at me for a couple of seconds before he said: 'It was an earthen-ware jar ... very old and possibly valuable. I decided to stick to it!'

'You were going to steal an empty jar?'

Grosset gave a derisive snort. 'Steal it, my crutch,' he said, somewhat inelegantly. 'Stealing is taking something belonging to someone else. The jar didn't belong to anyone; it had lain in the earth of Masada for damned near two thousand years, and no matter what the Yadins might say—*or* the bloody Department of Antiquities—it belonged to absolutely nobody until I found it . . . and then it belonged to me!'

Feeling a little like the local D.A., I asked why, if General Yadin didn't know about the jar there should be any fuss about it now? How could he possibly know a thing about the theft?'

'I don't actually know that he does,' said Grosset. 'I can only use my head and assume that he does . . . because, you see,' he said almost too casually, 'I didn't actually *take* the jar until a couple of weeks ago. That's why I came back to Israel, to get the damned thing. There was no time at the end of the last "dig", the bloody last bus out was practically honking at me, as it was. So I covered the thing and left it until I could come back . . . when Masada was practically deserted.'

'And you got it?'

He nodded. 'I got it!'

I still harped. 'Then how could they possibly . . .'

'Why the hell don't you listen? I've already told you that I have no way of telling whether they know or not, I can only expect that they do. You see, I was in a frantic hurry; there were workmen all over the bloody place. I heard someone shouting, whether at me or someone else I didn't wait to find out. I just grabbed the jar and bolted. It was only on the way down that I realised that I'd left the perfect give-away mould of the thing in the earth, for them to find. Now *that's* what I think they've discovered at Masada. They've found the shape and they'll know that nothing has been turned in . . . !' He left the rest—and it wasn't a great deal—to the imagination.

'But why connect you with the theft?'

'With the system they use at Masada,' he explained, 'they'll know damned well that nobody still on the job could have taken it . . . and they'll know that I'm here, sitting on my backside in Tel-Aviv. The Israelis didn't hack out a nation by playing the bloody fool, you know, Joyce. They can add up the score, and faster and better than most. So that if they've found that impression in the earth—and I think they have—it points in only one direction ... mine! And all because of that bloody stupid remark you had to make to Carmella Yadin this morning. It will have been reported, of course, and unless I'm wrong, you'll be under surveillance this minute ... if you haven't been already!'

I gave a jump. 'What do you mean by that?'

Grosset slowly grinned. 'I know damned well that I've had a watcher for nearly two weeks and, as we had a long, cosy chat the night you arrived, you could be suspected of being my accomplice. How d'you like them eggs, brother Joyce?'

I felt my skin crawling. We isolated, insular Australians read the books and see the films, happily dismissing it all as a romp and relegating the spies and secret agents to an amusing world of fantasy forgetting that, while James Bond certainly belongs there, John le Carre's grubby little man in the greasy raincoat rightly belongs on the seat next to us in the bus.

But there was another reason for my mobile goosepimples. Only two days before, someone had gone through my private papers in my hotel room. While this might have been no more than a snoopy housemaid, it is hardly likely that she would have played my tape recorder. On the other hand, it is equally unlikely that any trained 'spy' would have forgotten to rewind the spool. Perhaps, like Grosset retrieving that ancient jar at Masada, whoever it was didn't have time! Something the owlish archaeologist had said a couple of minutes back was nagging at me.

'Why did you say you wished to God you'd never seen Masada?' I asked. He stared at me but said nothing, so I decided to put it another way. 'No matter how much you regret the theft,' I said, 'why should you get so upset over an empty jar?

He drained his already empty glass and stood up, buttoning his coat. Looking down at me, he said it right to my face: 'Because the bloody thing wasn't empty, is why!' With his block-buster dropped, he turned and again headed for the golden elevators. It was the perfect exit!

A few minutes later, seeing spies at every table, I followed.

It was the next afternoon that I discovered that my new room had been 'bugged', which meant that the toilet in my old room had deliberately been blocked in order to justify a change into this one. Although I never found the 'bug' I soon had evidence that it was working perfectly.

Anticipating that it might take days for Menachem Begin to line up everything, I had begun to think of other ways of getting to Masada in the event that BOAC could not re-flight me to give Begin more time. As it stood, I was scheduled to fly out of Israel the following Monday night. Finding that Arkia Inland Airlines ran a light-plane service to Masada, I booked with the hotel concierge to fly there and back next day. After phoning to confirm that my booking was okay and that I was on the plane, he later called up to say that the flight had been cancelled 'because the airstrip is under repair'. In the height of the tourist season?

I blew hell out of him for telling me he already had the ticket, and stormed downstairs to blow him out some more. At the elevators I met one of a charming mysterious pair of twin sisters who'd been haunting me from my very first day in Israel.

Apparently their itinerary exactly coincided with mine ... which was curious because I had none! No matter where I went—deciding the place on the spur of the moment—that's where they'd turn up, too.

As she passed into the lift and the doors started to hiss closed, she called out: 'Tough luck about the plane!' There was only one way she could have known!

By Friday noon, I still hadn't heard from Mennahem Begin and all efforts to contact him at home or office—even through his PRO who was supposed to be 'handling' me—were ineffective. Time was running out and it was imperative that I delay my departure if ever I was to visit Masada. However, BOAC gave me no hope of another flight this side of Christmas—an impossible date—so that I was forced to stick to my original booking. This meant that unless Begin came good with a rush, I should have to get to Masada under my own steam, permit or no permit. At the moment, my 'steam' looked like being the trusty Dodge taxi of my guide, philosopher and very good friend—and the self-proclaimed 'best damned guide in all Israel'—Mordechai Zakai.

Saturday came and went, and still no news. I gave up and settled with Mordechai to drive the Masada the next morning (Sunday) and broke this news to Mennachem

Begin's PRO, Mrs. Livsha Jameson. To my astonishment this lady turned up at my hotel just as the taxi arrived next morning, with a most unusual request. There and then, she wanted me to inspect the 'Irgun' museum, even though she knew that my time was precious if I were to get to Masada and back that day.

Using as bait the offer to make one last desperate try to contact her boss, I gave in and wasted an hour—all for nothing—before I was free and able to set off for the legendary Masada at last.

We drove south to Beersheba and headed out into the Negev along a perfect road, passing by Bedouin ploughing with sharpened tree branches pulled by camels, vast acres of underground spray irrigation in the heart of the desert and Israel's Atomic City on the distant skyline, its fences carrying the familiar green clover-leaf warning of radiation. Coming at last to Sedom (Sodom) we turned sharp left by Lot's Wife and sped past fifty feet high dangerous cliffs of dirty green salt. At last, looming through a rain squall and looking rather like the stump of a decayed molar, we saw Masada. A few minutes later and we had parked by a complex of new stone buildings, although there wasn't a sign of the brown military tents in which the five hundred or more members of the expedition were supposed to live.

Puzzled, I asked for General Yadin ... and was told that we had come to the wrong place; that he and the expedition were camped on the same plateau from which General Silva had attacked Masada one thousand nine hundred years before. This was a thousand feet up and many convoluted miles away on the other side of the mountain. As it was then—thanks to Mrs. Jameson—3.30 p.m., all hope that I should set foot on Masada was forever gone.

Angrily pulling from my wallet the letter of permit refusal written by Mrs. Yadin, I pointed out where she had invited me to come the way I had come and to where she had directed me ... and, only too late realised that it had all been intended; that the spot she had chosen for me was at the very foot of the mountain and well and truly away from the camp. Obviously I was not meant to be able to 'badger' the General.

Only then, while rereading the letter, did I notice a very odd thing. Mrs. Yadin's refusal was dated 30 November—it had been received in Tel-Aviv, thirty miles away—by Mrs. Jameson a week later ... or so it was said. Something certainly seemed to be wrong with Israel's postal service ... or with something.

With the taximeter clanking away the quarter miles, we set off to return the 150 miles back to Tel-Aviv. Whoever it was: the Yadins, Menachem Begin or even the ghosts of Masada, someone certainly didn't want me on that mountain ... and looked like having won the battle. Well, we can't all be Romans!

Monday was a panic of packing, last minute calls, drinks and so on but, at about 6.30 p.m., all was ready to leave the Dan Hotel and head for the Airport, except for the formality of paying my bill. There was a crush around the desk in which I spotted Grosset, apparently doing the same thing ... which was curious because the desk had previously told me that no 'Professor Grosset' was registered. At the time, I hadn't thought much of the matter, assuming that—like many—he lived in some nearby *pension* and used the hotel's public rooms as a base. Yet, here he was, checking out! When I had set my affairs and so on in order and was free to tackle him about the mystery, he was gone.

However, one of the attractive twins was there, talking to a man wearing a black nylon raincoat with 'gold' fittings; Madison Avenue is—or was—thick with them like the measles. She and I exchanged farewells and I was on my way; about to shake the dust of 'that city' of Israel off my feet ... as Jesus had once advised his disciples to do in the case of any city refusing its help to a guest. Whatever mystery had surrounded my abortive attempt to get to Masada, it was over at last and no longer mattered; Grosset and his stolen jar of goodies and the whole ratpack of them could go take a running jump, I was free of them.

That's what *I* thought!

Within ten minutes of hitting Lod airport with the faithful Mordechai—whose honoured free guest I was for this drive out of the country—he suddenly dived into the crowd and, like a mastiff, emerged with ... Menachem Begin.

Smiles, handshakes and apologies. 'I'm sorry that I couldn't get you to Masada,' smiled the politician. 'I tried my best and hardest ... but my hands were tied!' That last sentence is still engraved upon my memory in letters of ice. What the hell was the man talking about? Before I could ask him, he was paged to an aircraft making a special flight to Jerusalem to enable him to attend some urgent Parliamentary crisis.

'Perhaps when you come back, Mr. Joyce—as I am sure you will—things will be very different!' Although I murmured something about 'They'd better be', I was still thinking about the second cliffhanger he'd tossed in sixty seconds flat. The man talked in riddles and, for all his smiling handshake, was not at his ease. With the loudhailers booming his name, he was gone ... his singing 'Shaloooom' drifting behind him like the aroma of a good cigar.

A very long time after this, needing corroboration of his part in the bizarre affair, I wrote to Menachem Begin and asked him to confirm the substance of what has been recounted here. There was no reply.

All that one has now to prove that we ever met is a copy of his book *The Revolt*, which he was gracious enough to inscribe with a long, personal and autographed dedication. One prizes it and hopes that he recalls the occasion.

After this excitement, Mordechai Zakai and I moved to the bars and, a few drinks later, said our farewells. Alone again, I walked back into the lounge as his tail-lights braked for the turn, and he was gone. Just inside the entrance, a big glass showcase claimed the attention. Gold, silver and bronze medallions commemorating both the excavation of Masada and the Jewish heroism which it proved, proudly boasted: 'Shall not Fall Again'. Well, that was true, if they meant me.

What the hell had they thought I was in Israel for, to steal it? I walked back into the lounge and, selecting an empty bench, flopped down—my cabin-bag at my feet—completely bushed.

How long I had been sitting there before I became aware of the man pacing nervously up and down, I simply don't know. A cursory glance told me that he was a total stranger yet he seemed to be looking at me every now and again as if to say that I should have known him. Suddenly, as if making up his mind, he swung towards the bench and sat down, plomping his cabin bag on the seat beside him. It was the twin of my own.

It was only then that I recognised Professor Grosset.

The big brown beard and the shaggy hair were gone; the thick, pebbled spectacles, too. The mildly eccentric, tweedy clothes he habitually wore were gone, and were now replaced by a smarly cut, dark grey flannel suit. He looked like just another overpaid executive doing the rounds of his international branches. The change was startling ... particularly as he had been the old, familiar Grosset when I had seen him paying his hotel bill only an hour or so earlier. Which reminded me that I had a bone to pick with him about his identity.

'For God's sake,' I started. 'What the hell have you done to yourself? And why?'

'I was hoping you wouldn't recognise me,' he smirked. 'In fact, when it took you so long, I thought I'd got away with it.'

'But what's the big idea? And what are you doing here? Are you off somewhere?'

The questions tumbled out in medicine cabinet style. He pulled from an inside pocket a blue BOAC Flight Voucher and flipped it open with insulting nonchalance.

'Flight 710,' he recited. 'Tel-Aviv to Delhi ... departing at 9.30 p.m. Monday 14 December in the year of Our Lord ...'

'But that's my flight!' I almost yelled.

Grosset yawned. 'It's a private plane, perhaps?'

I shrugged and mumbled something about having had no idea that he had proposed leaving Israel so soon. 'Anyway,' I finished, 'why Delhi? I should have thought that you'd have been heading for the good old U.S.A. and your Chair!'

'From Delhi,' he muttered, and he looked as sad as he sounded, 'one can go anywhere!'

I thought it an odd remark. I also thought he could go to hell and fry for all I cared. I came back to his faked identity. He was as balanced as a cat.

'A false name? Well, let's be practical, Joyce. In my position and engaged on my activity, you'd very probably have used a false name, too.'

'But what's your real name?' I pressed. 'Is it Grosset or is that the alias?'

'Suppose we leave that little matter until we're safely on the plane?'

There was something in his tone and his use of 'safely' which made me look at him, sharply.

'What do you mean by "safely"?'

He laid an arm on the bulging bag beside him. 'Let's just say that I think there's more than a rough chance that I might not make it!'

Suddenly, the drachma dropped. Immersed in my own troubles, I hadn't given a moment's conscious thought to Grosset's jar or its contents since our discussion the previous Wednesday night but, all at once, I knew!

A couple of years before I had read the late Edmund Wilson's Fontana paperback *The Scrolls From The Dead Sea* but had forgotten about it until then. In fact, my interest in scrolls was so minute that I had spent a whole afternoon sitting in the King David Hotel in Jerusalem reading Menachem Begin's book . . . when, had I been interested, I could have been standing in awe looking at the famous scrolls which were housed in the 'Dome of the Books' about a hundred yards away.

So Grosset had found a scroll jar which wasn't empty—and which certainly didn't contain peanut butter—and was smuggling it out of the country, the larcenous dog.

'If what you've got in that bag is what I think you've got in that bag,' I said, 'I've got the latest price on your chances of getting away with it, Chum—nil, followed by a couple of zeroes. The odds against it are astronomical!'

'Against me, they are,' he admitted, 'but not against . . . you! That's why I need your help!'

As I sat open-mouthed with astonishment at his cool nerve, he said the most wildly funny thing possible.

'Look here, it's not as though I'm asking you to do anything illegal. Please don't think that.'

'Oh, no,' I snorted, 'only about twenty years illegal, that's all. You're off your head, Professor. It's larceny on a grand scale.' Then, meaning the scroll or whatever it was inside the jar, I added: 'What's the thing worth, anyway?'

'Oh, about $5,000 American.'

'Good God,' I exploded. 'You'd risk going to the pokey for life, just for a miserable scroll worth a mere . . . ?'

'Not the scroll, you bloody fool; $5,000 is what the job is worth . . . to you!'

'That's not what I meant,' I snapped, 'and you damned well know it! What's the "thing" worth on the open market?'

'For what this is,' said the fake Professor Grosset, 'there's no open market. In fact, there's no market at all except for a doubtful one ... and I can't be certain that even this exists until I go there and find out. As it is, I'm taking a hell of a financial risk offering you so much!'

I told him to shove his money where the monkey hid the nuts; that I wasn't interested ... so he tried another tack.

'Look here, Joyce,' he wheedled. 'Don't you think the Israelis owe you something? They could have let you get your story material on Masada just by showing you a little simple courtesy and ...'

'And who,' I cut in, bitterly, 'is responsible for the fact that they didn't?'

Grosset went on regardless. 'Here you are ... you've come all the way around the world to get your story—or will have, by the time you get home tomorrow—and what have you got for all that money? A box of colour slides? Why go home empty-handed, when you don't have to?'

Put that way, it seemed to be a reasonable argument ... until I thought of an Israeli gaol. What I should have done at that moment was got up and walked away, but I didn't ... and was undone.

'Had I been kicked in the teeth as hard as you have,' he purred, 'I should welcome the chance to even up the score a bit. And you can ... by doing such a very little thing, really.'

'What's the little thing?'

His eyes didn't leave mine as he said: 'All you have to do is pick up this bag of mine instead of your own when we're paged to board the aircraft, walk past those two "goons" at the door to the tarmac ... and hop on board. I'll carry your bag and we'll swap back in the plane. So easy for luggage to get mixed up. Well, what do you say?'

It sounded so simple. Casually—or as casually as I could—I stood up and stretched. Over the heads of the crowd I could see two men standing chatting at the tarmac door ... or were they merely pretending to? ... while their eyes darted at the crowd.

To me, they were obvious. Men of their occupation look and 'smell' alike the whole world over, irrespective of nationality. Bad actors all, they tend to exaggerate their assumed innocence and so betray their guilt. The lounge of an International Airport is no place for jaunty nonchalance. This is where it's for real ... either the coming or the going; this is where the emotions are raw, naked and all too frequently bleeding; where the very air is whip-tight, and as brittle as lawn grass on a frosty morning. And here were these two 'goons' probably swapping dirty stories?

However, if anything else were needed to confirm Grosset's identification, they both wore black nylon raincoats with the swishy 'gold' fittings ... and one of them was the man I'd seen chatting to the beautiful twin at the Dan Hotel as I checked out.

'I'd never get away with it,' I told Grosset as I sat down. 'One of the chaps knows me; he saw me back at the Dan!'

'They both know me,' was his dry reply, 'But only as I was, not as I am now. That's why I made the transformation after I'd paid my bill; I expected them.'

'What makes you think it's you they're waiting for?'

'They came to the Dan just as I was leaving. I was waiting on the second floor for the elevator. When it came up, they got out. Without giving me a second glance, they went straight to my door. I heard them start knocking as I pressed the button ... damned hard, I can tell you!'

I asked him why he thought he couldn't walk past them unrecognised a second time?

'Maybe I could ... and could get away with it,' he conceded. 'But the point is ... I'm too damned scared to give it a fling!'

I still wasn't convinced and he knew it, so now he pulled out all the stops.

'Look, old man, forget *me* in this thing. It's truly not for my own sake that I'm asking; it's this scroll that's important. I've simply *got* to get it out of Israel tonight! I've got to!'

'You've been sitting on the bloody thing for a couple of weeks ... so why is it so urgent now?'

'Because that's the sort of scroll it is,' he said, quite simply. Oddly enough, they were the first words of his that sounded believable. I let him go on.

'It wasn't until last Friday that I knew for certain that it was authentic. Up until then, I was only backing my own judgment that it wasn't all kinds of a fake. The moment I knew that it wasn't, I was around at BOAC in five minutes flat, booking on this Flight. It was the first I could get on. Now that I know what the thing really is, I can't risk it being in Israel another hour.'

'Why not?'

'Because the bloody Israelis would shove it into the incinerator if they got their hands on it, is why!'

He launched into a long explanation of how, when he got back to Tel-Aviv from Masada with his loot, and had removed the scroll from the jar, he found it too dry and brittle to handle. Twenty centuries of bone dry desert heat had extracted all its natural moisture content and, before it would again be flexible enough to unroll, he had to replace some of the lost moisture by treating it in a make-shift humidifier he rigged up in his hotel bathroom. Only then could he make an estimate of its age, which he placed at somewhere in the 1st century A.D. Later, he was able to read its own 'date', but not even this was good enough.

He told me that he'd carefully cut off a portion of the unused end of the rolled parchment and had sent it to a discreet friend at the Hebrew Technion, the Israel Institute of Technology, at Haifa, asking him to arrange an urgent radio-carbon 14 test on it. Now I am in no position to know whether or not the Technion is equipped or able to undertake such a test; I am simply repeating what Grosset said. In any case, the plan might even have entailed the colleague sending the sample overseas for the test to be run. However that might be, Grosset told the tale with the utmost sincerity. It was a plausible story, but somehow . . . !

'Look here,' I said. 'How do I know that this isn't all a load of codswallop? For all I know to the contrary, this bag of yours that you want me to smuggle past those 'goons' might just as easily be stuffed with Herod the Great's golden regalia, or hashish or even polished diamonds, as this damned scroll you're so glib about. So, before we say another word about "will I or won't I?", suppose you show me the thing? Just so I'll be sure it's there!'

He sat thinking for a moment or two then, grabbing his bag, stood up and headed for the men's lavatories. And I followed him.

Luckily, the place was empty when we entered and we both squeezed into a cubicle and shut the door. After a lot of trouble with a faulty zip on his bag, he finally got it open and, with me holding it, reached inside and lifted out an object wrapped in a towel stolen from the Dan Hotel. It was slightly damp and I wanted to know why.

'The only thing I could think of for moisture control until we get to Delhi,' explained Grosset. 'Now you peel off the towel while I hold the scroll . . . careful!'

As carefully as I could, I unfolded the towel and at last saw the object of the exercise.

It consisted of a rolled up length of tatty brown parchment made of separate sheets which had been stitched edge to edge to make a roll of—as near as I could guess—ten or twelve feet long. Each 'page' would have been in the vicinity of about nine inches by five inches. Unevenly rolled up, it had a hollow centre and tattered edges. Its visible end—the outside loop—was much darker than the rest and was mottled or marbled by a mould of some kind. I wasn't terribly impressed, and said so.

'You'd better be. Take a bloody good look, Joyce, because you'll never get another chance. Only three men have ever set eyes on this, and you and I are two of them. The third—the man who wrote it—died exactly 1,891 years ago. How does that grab you, eh?'

I stared at the thing. It didn't grab me at all.

'Hold out your hands, you bloody Philistine; I'm about to honour you with an experience you'll never forget.' He put the scroll into my outstretched palms. 'Drop it and I'll cheerfully kill you, you bugger!' With very careful fingers, he eased back a loop of parchment to reveal neat rows of black lettering which, to me, appeared to be as legible as the day they were written.

'Hebrew?'

'Aramaic,' he said. 'Much the same thing to the layman. Aramaic was . . .' He broke off as someone came into the lavatory. We stood there, making no sound, until the intruder had completed his errand and was gone. As soon as it was safe to speak, Grosset said: 'You don't realise it of course, but what you are holding in your hands is probably the most astounding document that has ever existed!'

'What about the Dead Sea Scrolls?'

He laughed, softly. 'Compared with this, the best of the Dead Sea Scrolls is an unimportant scribble. This is a personal document . . . a letter . . . addressed to nobody . . . bearing the name or signature if you like . . . of a man whom many say never lived. It was written at Masada and actually describes the imminent fall of the fortress. It was written the night before that happened which the author identified as the "eve of the Sabbath". So if our unreliable historian friend Josephus is to be trusted, we can definitely date this scroll to the night of 15 April A.D. 73. What do you think of that? Will anybody still be reading your piddling words a couple of thousand years from now? I doubt it!'

'Oh, I don't know! Who wrote the thing?'

Grosset held out the towel. 'Lay it carefully here,' he commanded. I watched as he tenderly rewrapped it and, stooping, put it back in the bag. This time I got a good look at what else was in there, and Grosset knew it.

'The shards of pottery,' he explained, 'are the remains of the jar. I had the bad luck to drop it in the bathroom. Those other things . . .'

'. . . are crampons,' I finished for him. 'I've wondered how the hell you got to the top of Masada without being spotted. You didn't use either of the paths, you went straight up the side, like a bloody cat, with those mountaineering crampons on your feet, you cunning stoat!'

He nodded, and smiled. 'Something like that,' he said as he zipped up his bag and motioned for me to open the door. Outside, I started rinsing the dust of the ancient past from my hands . . . or was it fear of some Tutenkhamen-like 'curse'? He caught me looking at him in the mirror, or did I catch him?

'Well, what's it to be, old man? Will you do it?'

Where's the harm, I thought. After all, he had found the thing and had risked his life to get it . . . and was risking God knows what else to keep it.

'Yes,' I said, briskly. 'I'll do it, but not for the money, I'm no man's hired hand. Just tell me who wrote it, and I'll carry your damned bag aboard that plane just for the sheer hell of the thing.'

Now that he had got his own way, the archaeologist was a new man. His gloom vanished. 'After this, Joyce old man . . . I'm your friend for life. Ask me anything you want and it's yours, no matter what it . . .'

'Who wrote it?'

When he still hesitated, I pressed harder.

'Come *on*, Grosset. Do you want the deal or don't you?'

'Who wrote it?' He stood there blinking a moment before saying anything. At last he said: 'You're not going to believe this, of course, nobody will believe it. They'll say it's an impossible fake and a fraud but . . . here, read this.'

He pulled out his wallet and unfolded a badly written

note in English, dated from Haifa almost a week before. Baldly, it stated that the radio-carbon 14 test carried out on the scroll sample sent by Grosset computed its age as being within the date-range of 30 B.C. to 170 A.D. Allowing for an error of plus or minus 100 years, the likely date when the animal whose skin provided the parchment was killed, was somewhere about 70 A.D. Very thoughtfully, I refolded the note and handed it back to Grosset.

'Near enough to the date of Masada's fall, wouldn't you say, old man? As to the author ... well, he was a man who had cut himself off from the world for many years; a man whose son had been captured by the Romans and crucified before his eyes. With his son dead, and his own death probably only an hour away, the scroll author announces the end of the High Priest-Kings of Israel, of whom he claims to have been the last direct descendant. These, Joyce, were the Hasmonean kings or, as you probably know them better, the Maccabeans. So, old boy, you'd better face it; the author was, in fact, King of Israel!'

Despite my then lack of knowledge about the history of Judea, I shivered and my scalp prickled with excitement, but I didn't dare interrupt, even had there been anything to say.

'But this man was something more than King,'—and now Grosset's voice took on an almost elegiac tone—'He was an old man—as he himself puts it, "son of nearly eighty years"—and thus he had lived almost twice as long as his father, Jacob. He gives his own name as ... Jesus of Gennesareth!'

Mis-hearing the last word, I exploded.

'But, my God, Grosset, you're crazy! It's impossible!'

He stopped me with an uplifted hand. 'What is crazy about it, my friend, is that for practically two thousand years the world has known the same man as ... Jesus of Nazareth!'

All I could do was stare at the man, and babble something about Jesus' father having been Joseph.

'The same gospels also claim that his father was God, so that, apparently, there's some confusion!'

The initial shock over, I began to get a grip on myself again. 'But for God's sake ... if Jesus were crucified in— what was it—30 A.D. or something like that, how could he possibly have been alive forty years later? How, Grosset?'

'Well, old boy, there *was* the Resurrection, wasn't there?' He stooped to pick up his bag as two men in a hurry surged in. He held open the door for us to pass through into the lobby. 'Makes you think, doesn't it?'

I had just thought of another objection when the loudhailers started clattering in rapid Hebrew. While the lounge was still echoing with Jewish groans, the speakers changed gear into English. Grosset's face was white. He spoke Hebrew, of course.

'Attention please! Passengers on BOAC Flight 710 from London to Melbourne via Zurich, Tel-Aviv, Teheran, Delhi, Rangoon, Singapore, Darwin and Sydney are advised that this flight has been delayed at Zurich and will be eight hours late in arriving at Tel-Aviv. The new arrival time is 5 a.m. tomorrow. Thank you!'

Now the non-Jewish sent up their groans and supplications to God Almighty. I turned to Grosset to protest that this was a hell of a way to run an airline, and found him now red faced and angry. Also, I think, frightened.

'This is the end of everything,' he raved. 'The bastards have got me ... do you see what they've done? They've pulled a few strings in London ... that aircraft's being deliberately delayed in Zurich to give them more time to find me ... !'

I advised him to stop being a bloody fool and to calm down; that it meant nothing of the kind. I told him that there had been heavy snow in Zurich when I had passed through two weeks before. For a moment he seemed to calm down, but when the loudhailers opened up again, to announce that delayed passengers would be accommodated at a nearby hotel at the airline's expense, he was on the verge of panic. He went right over the edge when he heard: 'Those passengers wanting accommodation are asked to line up at the desk and present their tickets!'

SWOOSH!

'It's a bloody trick,' he stormed. 'Line up all those for the hotel and identify yourselves! Oh, no, not me! You can do what you like about it, but me, I'm off!'

And, as ungrammatically as that, so he was! With that fantastic scroll in his bag, he turned and ran for the street. Hurrying after him as best I could, I was just in time to see his taxi pull away. He gave me a wave ... and was gone.

And never, as far as I could absolutely swear to it, did I ever see Professor Max Grosset again!

After a night of sleep in snoozes, tossing and turning, and of smoking-out the riddle of Grosset, the scroll and of all the strange events which had surrounded, involved and finally engulfed me during the past two weeks, I was jerked fully awake by the strident jangle of the phone. The aircraft had picked up time and would now be ready for takeoff at 4 a.m. Everybody up!

It was a thoroughly miserable bunch of bleary-eyeds which climbed into the waiting microbus for the ride back to the airport, which was strangely quiet and practically deserted compared with last night's bustle.

There was no trouble or fuss. A quick cup of coffee and we presented our boarding passes—issued the previous night—then wearily staggered up the steps into the 'Comet'.

As far as can be remembered, there were no formalities of any kind. One forgets whether Passports were stamped 'Departed'—an unfortunate word for air travellers—on the morning of our takeoff or the previous night; certainly mine bears the date of 15 December. However, there was no Custom's inspection. The men in the black nylon raincoats were gone—or not yet awake—and, in the event, Grosset could have smuggled out a hundred scrolls. What an opportunity he had missed. Or had he?

The doors whined shut, the jets burst into the familiar screaming rage which would sustain their fury all the way to distant Teheran ... and we were off.

Shalom, Israel!

As the lights of Lod winked of ancient secrets beneath our tilted wing, I fell asleep, knowing at last that I had been a stranger in a strange land. Teheran came and went in the morning, leaving only a memory of dirty yellow snow, a female lavatory attendant in the Men's, and of hundreds of olive-green Soviet made tanks parked in neat rows by the runway's end.

Late on a golden afternoon, we chased our shadow across an emerald India in which, standing like a herd of grazing elephant, were dozens of ancient temples, and slipped at last on to the long, black smear that was Palam Airport. We had arrived at Delhi!

It was only then that I remembered that it was to here that Professor Grosset had intended fleeing with his scroll;

that this was the place from which 'one can go anywhere!'
The remark was soon to have a strange significance.

Emotionally drained and physically exhausted by the
events and the long flight, I heard with complete indiffer-
ence that only disembarking passengers would be permitted to leave the aircraft. For forty minutes the rest of us
stayed in our seats as the plane was sprayed and refuelled,
while Customs Inspectors removed the aisle flooring, presumably in search of smuggled gold.

The most curious thing of all was, however, that here at
Delhi I might have got my last ever glimpse of Professor
Grosset and his black bag. Naturally I had assumed that,
as I hadn't seen him at the airport early that morning, he
had either been arrested or had decided that the plane was
too risky; that he would try to get out of Israel by other
means. However, there was no way of being sure; certainly I hadn't sighted him at Lod or aboard the aircraft,
but he might very well have been tucked away in the First
Class section, out of bounds to us lesser pinchpennies.

As chance had it, disembarking at Delhi were friends of
mine from Australia, an advertising tycoon named Leo
Glick, and his wife and party, on their way to see the Taj
Mahal by moonlight. Straining to give them a wave from
the window, I spotted a familiar grey-suited figure striding
from beneath the plane carrying a black cabin bag. The
man wasn't in my range of vision any more than a couple
of seconds—perhaps five—but it was long enough for me
to be ninety per cent certain that it was Professor Grosset
whom I saw.

If it were he, one is unable to explain how he came to
be aboard except as has already been suggested, although
there is one other possibility. Determined to get that scroll
out of Israel that night—with or without my help—he
might have loitered near the Airport until the plane arrived and, already having his checked ticket and boarding
pass from the previous night—as did all of us—simply
joined the tail-end of the queue going up the steps. And
who was there to stop him? The one great objection to
this theory has already been mentioned; my own Passport
is stamped for exit on 15 December and, one would
imagine, Grosset's must also have been presented and
stamped that morning.

Perhaps he had decided, after all, to run whatever
gauntlet there was at the Airport and had behaved no dif-

ferently from the rest of us. That there were no visible security men on duty that early morning might have been
entirely due to a snafu by some clerk ... who had failed
to advise Security of the new and earlier takeoff time. It
might have been Grosset's really lucky day.

Grosset or not—and subsequent events dissolve the uncertainty—another sight at Palam airport not only suggested what he might have been doing at Delhi but gave
piquancy to his remark: 'from Delhi one can go anywhere!',
for it seems to be a reasonable assumption that Delhi was
not his final destination.

Standing on the parking apron almost alongside our
'Comet' was another passenger aircraft bearing a band of
strange Cyrillic letters along the fuselage. It was, of
course, a Soviet Union Aeroflot 'Ilyushin'. Its midship
door was open and standing gazing morosely down the
landing-steps as he waited for customers, was a white-
jacketed, nose-picking steward. One got the distinct impression that the aircraft was either ready to receive its
passengers or, having loaded them already, was standing
waiting for the last one. Could it have been waiting for
our Flight to arrive with Professor Grosset?

As has already been mentioned, events reported in the
world's press during 1967 and since, strongly suggest that
the 'fifteenth' scroll might have, in fact, reached the Soviet
Union. If so, only Grosset could have taken it there. He
had said to me at Lod: 'There's no market at all (for the
scroll) except a doubtful one ... and I can't be certain
until I go there that even that exists!' Had he been referring to the Soviet Union? Why would reputedly Godless
Russia be interested in acquiring a document alleged to
have been written by the Jesus of Christianity?

Proved authentic, the scroll might have been considered
a most valuable weapon and one which might well be
turned to considerable political advantage.

Naturally enough, little of the foregoing can ever be
more than speculations and suspicions, for no matter how
true they might be, it is unlikely that they can ever be
proved. In any case, we are far too close to the events to
see them with the hindsight of history which, we are told,
reveals all ... or all that's fit to be told.

History might well decide that it was in the late sixties
of the 20th century that the Christian Church—having
been around for a long time, and determined to be around

for a long time to come—bowed like the pliant bamboo before the storm and, when it passed, sprang upright ... stronger than ever, but not quite the same.

It might even record the fact that the storm was caused by a strange document called the 'fifteenth' scroll.

The Credibility of Grosset's Claims

In testing the bogus 'Professor Grosset's' story for credibility—which we propose to do—the present author's must also come under scrutiny and, frankly, one wouldn't want it any other way. Naturally there will be many who, unable to accept the sheer enormity of the scroll's implications for their Faith, will not only claim that Grosset was a fake and a liar, but will even deny that he ever existed; that he is merely a character in a devised fiction which has been presented as fact.

To deal with the last charge first, and so to get it out of the way: my own credibility cannot be resolved on my own proclamation, so that until the march of events proves it, one way or the other, any discussion on it seems pointless.

However, it would be unlikely that any writer would devise such a story and back it up with five years of heartbreaking research and writing—refusing all other assignments and thereby sacrificing at least $50,000—merely on the off-chance of selling a book. Moreover, what has to be fitted to such a theory is the strange and plainly evident fact that the Grosset story fits like the proverbial glove. Also to be explained is why a writer who previously knew nothing of the Christian religion or its history beyond that learned in Sunday-school, would spend years devoted to becoming something of an adept in various areas which, normally, are the provinces of the experts, knowing that the story and conclusions would eventually be required to stand up to extremely critical examination, warts and all.

However, perhaps the best immediate test of the author's credibility might be first to test Professor Grosset's, remembering that, for a start, his name is an admitted fake.

In March 1967, the author wrote a long and detailed letter to General Yigael Yadin seeking information about

'Grosset' and disclosing as much of the affair as was then considered discreet. In addition, the letter asked for the reason why he was excluded from the Masada site in 1964, and raised at least one archaeological query about it which might have been expected to result in some comment. Here is General Yadin's reply in full:

> 47 Ramban Street,
> Jerusalem.
> 1st April 1967

Dear Mr. Joyce:

Thank you for your letter of 21st March '67. There was no Professor Grosset in the Masada team at any time and the other characteristics you give could fit scores of volunteers.

Moreover the entire story of the scroll is fantastic, and anyone with a little knowledge of scrolls and conditions in which they were discovered at Masada would have immediately detected the nonsense in the story.

I cannot here go into technical details of why this is so and I reserve these if necessary, for future comments on your book, should I be asked about it.

> Yours sincerely
> (signed) Yigael Yadin.

Well, you would be entitled to say, that's it! The whole affair was a hoax from start to finish! General Yadin is the expert, and that's what he practically says. The news that the whole thing might have been a hoax comes as no news to me. However, there are two things against the supposition that it was. Firstly, where is the point in such a hoax? Too many imponderables stood between its generation and a perpetrator's big laugh for it to have been even remotely likely. While the scroll might have been a fake, it would seem to have been of very ancient vintage and none of Grosset's making. Secondly, had Grosset been the hoaxer, why would he offer the victim $5,000? Just for a hell of a big laugh?

General Yadin is an expert in a number of fields and a man of impressive accomplishments. As an archaeologist and scholar he is rightly held in the highest respect. In fact, one would be fortunate to have him as a witness, so that I am happy to discover that—however unwittingly— he has become mine ... apparently against himself, as will soon be shown.

In the meantime, it must be confessed that his news that no 'Professor Grosset' was a member of the Expedition comes as no surprise. The man could have used any name he wished—even, probably, his real one—and still have been at Masada as one of the more than five thousand people who worked there between late 1963 and early 1965. As General Yadin's denial—unreservedly accepted in the context in which it was made—cannot be extended to cover the above possibility, Grosset's claim is not disproved and must therefore stand as valid until proved false.

As to the remainder of his reply, General Yadin's somewhat contemptuous dismissal of a report about what might yet prove to be an amazing literary antiquity, suggests that some tender sensitivities might have been flicked. Surely any lead, no matter how nonsensical it might appear, is worth some little investigation when it is alleged that one's pocket might have been picked of a valuable treasure? The author offered to answer any question the General might care to ask about the matter. There was none. Nor, it will have been noticed, was there any explanation of the ban placed on me visiting Masada, not even a repetition of that originally given by him. It seems a strange silence which might still have been too delicate to break.

One thing is certain about that ban; it was not imposed for the stated or any ordinary reason. If the combined efforts of the influential Menachem Begin and the then Prime Minister of Israel could not get it lifted, there had to be a very unusual reason why that was so. As Begin told me the night of my departure: '. . . my hands were tied!'

It is the second paragraph of General Yadin's letter, however, which is found to be the most intriguing, for in it he says: 'Moreover, the entire story of the scroll is fantastic, and anyone with a little knowledge of scrolls and conditions in which they were discovered at Masada would have immediately detected the nonsense in the story.'

Well, suppose we see how much 'nonsense' there *is* in Grosset's story. Suppose we call General Yadin as our expert witness to prove that the story is *not* quite the nonsense his letter says.

What did Grosset claim? That he had been a member of the Yadin Masada Expedition. We have shown that he could have been. Next, he claimed to have been working alone and to have discovered a scroll jar somewhere on the mountain; he never said where, precisely. He further claimed that he went back later and retrieved it, was interrupted by a workman calling out, and to have taken-off with his loot, forgetting in his hurry to erase the indentation it had left in the earth. He took it back to Tel-Aviv, removed the scroll from the jar, replaced some of its lost moisture content in a makeshift humidifier, unrolled it and read it. These would seem to be the only relevant points for discussion, as the General clearly was not interested in the scroll's contents. This, then, is what he described as nonsense. Now let us hear his testimony as culled from his own excellent book *Masada* (Weidenfeld & Nicolson) and which is to be recommended.

In that book General Yadin discloses that members of the Masada team did work alone on many occasions and that, in fact, it was a solo operator who found one of the fourteen scrolls discovered in the ruins, and turned it in.

Grosset would seem to have scored another point of credibility; which makes two!

As General Yadin admits that fourteen scrolls—or portions of them—were discovered to his knowledge, can he categorically deny that there was a fifteenth, of which he was unaware? This, I think, makes three points to Grosset.

According to the testimony of the General's book, all scroll discoveries made at Masada concerned material buried in the earth or under rubble with no protective wrapping and certainly no container. They were thus subject to decay and the rains of almost twenty centuries which, in that area, can be torrential. Incredibly, these fourteen had survived their long journey through time . . . so why should not Grosset's scroll have done the same? Particularly is this so as it was snug inside its protective jar and, for all we know to the contrary, might also have been in a dry cave instead of out in the open weather, as were the other fourteen. Its chances of survival were, in fact, a thousand times better than those of the others. I rather think that this is another point to Grosset, making four straight hits . . . and no misses.

What now calls for comment is the likely condition of Grosset's scroll, forgetting my own testimony on this score for my credibility is not established.

On General Yadin's evidence, most—though not all—of

the scroll material officially found at Masada was entirely illegible and could not be read by the naked eye owing to the parchment having weathered to an overall black, which obscured the writing. Not surprising in view of the conditions in which they were found. To counteract this, recourse was had to infra-red photography, which clearly revealed the writing in the developed prints and so enabled the documents to be read.

Grosset claimed—and for what it's worth, I support him—that the writing on his scroll was perfectly legible the moment he unrolled it. Why doubt him when at least one of the other Masada found scrolls was apparently in the same readable condition? His was better preserved. Why doubt him when the celebrated 'Isaiah' scroll found with the first batch of Dead Sea Scrolls was, again reportedly, in the same condition. It, too, was found in a cave ... out of the weather. Another point to Grosset's credibility? What's the total now? Five ... for none against!

The problem of unrolling has already been referred to and Grosset's method of overcoming the fragility of this super-dry old parchment has already been described to the extent that it is known. However, that this was not always the problem is revealed by another scroll expert, John Allegro, in his *The Dead Sea Scrolls* (Pelican. 1964 edition). Having been 'Keeper of the Scrolls' for King Hussein of Jordan's predecessor at the time these famous parchments emerged from their caves, he ought to know what he is talking about.

On page 19 of that book Allegro states that the exultant Bedouin who made the finds took one of the very first of the big scrolls to come to light, back to their camp and, there and then, unrolled it in their tent. 'It stretched,' wrote Allegro, 'from one end of the tent to the other.' Obviously, it must have been in an immediately pliable condition and in no need of hydration.

From all this—six points having been recorded it Grosset's favour and none against—it must be obvious that we have rapidly drawn away from General Yadin's area of 'fantastic ... nonsense' into one in which Grosset's story seems to have been distinctly possible. Strangest of all is that it is General Yadin's own evidence against himself which is mainly responsible.

The bogus one—and bogus he was in name, although he might well have been what he said he was, if not whom—claimed to have used mountaineering crampons in scaling Masada. These are steel frames which strap on to the soles of stout boots.

Expert opinion strongly argues that crampons would have been useless on Masada's soft stone. Be this as it may, Grosset had crampons in his bag and led me to believe he had used them. In the event, however, they might have proved as useless as the expert declares.

His claim to have been disturbed by workmen appears to have been possible, too, for General Yadin reveals that a few maintenance men were left working on the plateau right through the long, hot summer between the two excavation seasons of 1964.

So, to sum up Grosset's proposition in a few words, everything he claimed to have done, he could have done. This, of course, is not the same as saying that he actually did those things. However, all that we have been investigating here is the feasibility of his claims and that, one submits, has been conclusively proved.

Examination of the evidence through the screen of General Yadin's expert and published testimony suggests that he might have been too hasty in his abrupt dismissal of that 'fifteenth' scroll.

There have been many astonishing instances in recent years to prove that you can't trust everybody; that even the most perfect security measures can be breached.

Generally, the immediate reaction of authority to the suggestion that someone might have made a mockery of defences thought impregnable, is to deny that they have, in fact, been penetrated. The fact that the sad truth eventually emerges suggests that this unwillingness to face up to what has happened is sometimes carried far beyond a reasonable point and, sometimes, to the stage where recantation becomes impossible, even if desirable. This frequently results in officialdom denigrating both the evidence and the witness.

There is no doubt in my mind that hiding behind the bogus 'Professor Max Grosset' is probably a respected—and perhaps eminent—scholar and archaeologist who, if he took that scroll to its suspected destination, is possibly no longer with us; at least, not with any great degree of freedom. Those who feel obligated to disagree should keep a sharper eye on their newspapers. They might even be surprised at the capers eminent scholars—and even Christian clerics of stature—have got up to in purusit of the sport known as 'scroll-duggery', which is no more than the conversion of other people's ancient manuscripts into piles of lovely loot. My next book devotes a chapter to it.

Men are merely men and are subject to the very same temptations which beset us all from time to time though, perhaps, scholars and clerics should be better equipped than most to resist them. That most do, is beside the point ... which is that, as the record will show, Grosset—whoever he really was—wouldn't have been the first of his profession to have met Beelzebub.

Strangely enough, as our utterly reliable gospels report, it was in just about the Masada area of the Wilderness of Judea that Jesus of Nazareth—or was it Jesus of Gennesareth?—is reputed to have met the very same gentleman. He lost out, too!

Bibliography

Desirable though it might be thought by some, no complete list of sources can be given, for none was kept. As the research upon which this book has been based extended over several years, occurred in many places and concerned public as well as private libraries, much of it was 'done on the run' and such references as might have been noted at the time, are just not available without going through the whole process all over again. Thus, I hope I shall be forgiven; in any case, most scholars will know the sources while laymen will find a search most rewarding. However, what I can do is list a number of works which have all played a part in the putting together of this book and these, too, can reward the interested reader.

Objections to Christian Belief, MacKinnon, Vidler, Williams and Bezzant, Pelican, 1967

The Death of Jesus, Joel Carmichael, Pelican, 1966.

The Passover Plot, Hugh J. Schonfield, Hutchinson, 1965.

The Apocrypha of the Old Testament, Standard Revised Version, Nelson, 1962.

Was Jesus Married?, William E. Phipps, Harper & Row, 1970.

The Birth of the Christian Faith, James McLeman, Oliver & Boyd, 1962.

The Historical Geography of the Holy Land, George Adam Smith, Fontana, 1966.

The Dead Sea Scrolls and Primitive Christianity, Jean Danielou, Mentor-Omega, 1962.

The Meaning of the Dead Sea Scrolls, A. Powell Davies, New American Library, 1961.

The Scrolls from the Dead Sea, Edmund Wilson, Fontana, 1962.

The Dead Sea Scrolls, John Allegro, Penguin, 1964.

Josephus, the Jewish War, Trans. G. A. Williamson, Penguin, 1959.

Jerusalem & Rome (The Writings of Josephus), Nahum N. Glatzer, Fontana, 1966.

The Secret Sayings of Jesus (Gospel of Thomas), Grant & Freedman, Fontana, 1960.

The Life of Jesus, Marcello Craveri, Panther, 1967.

Mainsprings of Civilisation, Ellsworth Huntington, Mentor, 1959.

The Anvil of Civilisation, Leonard Cottrell, Mentor, 1963.

Jews, God and History, Max I. Dimont, New American, 1962.

Masada, Yigael Yadin, Weidenfeld & Nicolson, 1966.

Dictionary of the Bible, Edit. James Hastings, Clark, 1905.

Dictionary of Christ & the Gospels, Edit. James Hastings, Clark, 1908.

and, of course,
The Holy Bible.

Other MENTOR Titles of Special Interest

☐ **HOW TO KNOW GOD: THE YOGA APHORISMS OF PATANJALI** translated with Commentary by Swami Prabhavananda and Christopher Isherwood. This classic work on yoga, its goal and methods, is essential to an understanding of Hindu religious practice. For more than fifteen hundred years the writings of Patanjali have been a principal influence on Hindu spiritual exercises. Index. (#MQ1230—95¢)

☐ **THE MEANING OF THE GLORIOUS KORAN: An Explanatory Translation** by Mohammed Marmaduke Pickthall. The complete sacred book of Mohammedanism, translated with reference to scholarship. (#MW1195—$1.25)

☐ **THE LIVING TALMUD: THE WISDOM OF THE FATHERS AND ITS CLASSICAL COMMENTARIES** selected and translated by Judah Goldin. A new translation, with an illuminating essay on the place of the Talmud in Jewish life and religion. (#MQ1024—95¢)

☐ **THE ETERNAL MESSAGE OF MUHAMMED** by Abd-al-Rahman Azzam, translated by Caesar E. Farah. A renowned Arab statesman and scholar examines the modern Muslim state as he outlines the origin, development, and philosophy of the Islamic religion. (#MT634—75¢)

More SIGNET and MENTOR Books
of Related Interest

☐ **WHAT THE GREAT RELIGIONS BELIEVE by Joseph Gaer.**
An enlightening account of the basic beliefs of the
world's historic religions—Hinduism, Jainism, Christianity, Islam, Zoroastrianism, Confucianism, Judaism,
and Zen Buddhism and others—with selections from
their sacred literature. Bibliography. (#Y6172—$1.25)

☐ **HOW THE GREAT RELIGIONS BEGAN (revised) by
Joseph Gaer.** A comparison of the differences and similarities in each religion, underscoring the spirit of
brotherhood and peace that is the basic principle of all
faiths.   (#Q4739—95¢)

☐ **VARIETIES OF RELIGIOUS EXPERIENCE by William
James.** A new edition of James' classic work on the
psychology of religion and the religious impulse.
(#MW1267—$1.50)

☐ **THE SERMON ON THE MOUNT According to Vedanta by
Swami Prabhavananda.** A fascinating and superbly enlightening Hindu reading of the central gospel of Christianity by the renowned author of books on Indian
religious philosophy.   (#MY1150—$1.25)

☐ **THE MEANING OF THE DEAD SEA SCROLLS by A.
Powell Davies.** A fascinating interpretation of one of
the most important archaeological discoveries of recent
times; the finding of ancient documents which revolu-
tionize religious teachings and beliefs.
(#MY1328—$1.25)